What's Not to Love?

Also by Jonathan Ames

I Pass Like Night

The Extra Man

What's Not to Love?

The Adventures of a Mildly Perverted Young Writer

Jonathan Ames

Crown Publishers
New York

Much of this book originally appeared in the *New York Press* in slightly different form. "The Playboys of Northern New Jersey" appeared in *Word*. Some of the names have been changed in deference to friends and subjects.

The *New York Times* article on
page 199 has been reprinted with permission. Copyright © 1998 by the New York Times Co.

Published by Crown Publishers, New York, New York
Member of the Crown Publishing Group
Random House, Inc. New York, Toronto, London, Sydney, Auckland
www.randomhouse.com

CROWN is a trademark and the Crown colophon is a registered trademark of Random House, Inc.

Printed in the United States of America

Design by Susan Maksuta

Library of Congress Cataloging-in-Publication Data
Ames, Jonathan.
What's not to love?: the adventures of a mildly perverted young writer / by Jonathan Ames.
1. Ames, Jonathan—Homes and haunts—New York (State)—New York.   2. City and town life—New York (State)—New York—Humor.   3. New York (N.Y.)—Social life and customs—20th century.   4. Authors, American—20th century.   I. Title.
PS3551.M42 Z475 2000
813'.54—dc21   99-055758

ISBN 0-609-60514-3

10 9 8 7 6 5 4 3 2 1

First Edition

For Patrick Bucklew

ACKNOWLEDGMENTS

The author would like to express his appreciation and gratitude to Jennifer Hunt, Doug Pepper, Rosalie Siegel, Russ Smith, John Strausbaugh, and Ben Xavier.

CONTENTS

Contents

III. DIFFICULTIES

What's Not to Love?

PROLOGUE

Dear Kind Reader,

If you are standing in a bookstore glancing at this, I'm sorry that the first thing you have to come across is an introduction—a writer's equivalent of a throat-clearing, and not a very good selling point. But I thought you should know that this book, in a serialized, Dickens-like fashion, first appeared in a newspaper, a weekly Manhattan journal called the *New York Press.* I've been working for this paper for the last three years, and initially I wrote a story about every six weeks on such compelling topics—to give but two examples—as my traumatically delayed puberty and an unfortunate encounter with crabs. And I'm not referring, I'm afraid, to tasty Maryland crabs.

This kind of crusading reportage went on for about a year, and then in October of 1997, I began to contribute more regularly, penning a bi-weekly column, a chronicle of my adventures, called "City Slicker." At first, I had thought of calling the column "The Onanist." The idea was, of course, to attract attention, but ultimately I didn't want to pigeonhole myself.

So every two weeks—under deadline—I have to come up with an adventure to fill "City Slicker," and this is not always easy. Thus, I often look for escapades from my past to meet my quota of columns. And so what has emerged from all the writing I've done for the paper over three years is a sort of life story (for that phrase I admit to stealing liberally from Graham Greene's autobiography, *A Sort of Life*)—a story that I have taken and placed in the book you are holding at this very moment.

And now I must apologize for all this literary name-dropping. It's terrible the way I try to create lofty parallels between myself and great writers—Greene, Dickens. And, furthermore, if you turn back to the contents page, you'll see that I dare to make references to the Bible, Sophocles, Dante, Milton, F. Scott Fitzgerald, Thomas Mann, Jackie Mason, Edmund Rostand, Isaac Bashevis Singer, J. M. Synge, and J.R.R. Tolkien. So this is all an outrage and I should be properly lashed. If you like, you can contact me care of the publisher and we'll try to arrange a public flogging, perhaps at a Barnes & Noble or the 92nd Street Y.

In any event, if you're standing in a bookstore reading this introduction and you don't feel the need to press on, I mildly—I don't want to be too much of a huckster or self-promoter—urge you to turn to the official first page. It's probably more amusing, and perhaps even enticing enough to get you to continue reading. At least I hope so.

With only good intentions,
Jonathan Ames
New York City

I
Troubles

Pubertas Agonistes

I STARTED PUBERTY VERY LATE. I was nearly sixteen. And for complicated reasons this late arrival of my puberty caused me to stop playing competitive tennis. But before my puberty problem, I had trouble with my lower back and with my left testicle.

The back was the first thing to go—in the third grade, at an introductory Cub Scout picnic. I had gone to this picnic against my better judgment. I must have heard some rumors about the Cub Scouts and I was afraid that I would have to build things at the picnic and use tools, and I already knew by the third grade that I wasn't mechanically inclined. I put up as much resistance as an eight-year-old could—there may have been some tears—but my father insisted that we go. And as it turned out there were no tools at the picnic, only game-playing. I started having a pleasant tennis ball catch with another boy, and after several tosses the ball sailed over my head. I went to retrieve it, and though I thought I was all right, I must have still been nervous about joining the Cub Scouts, because when I bent over to pick up the ball, I experienced terrible spasms in my lower back. It was crippling, the muscles clenched like fingers into fists, and I folded up and fell to the ground. My father had to carry me out of the picnic past all the other boys and their fathers. I remember him laying me in the backseat of the car.

This was upsetting for my dad: He was a former Boy Scout. He had hoped that I would become an Eagle Scout one day, a goal he had been unable to achieve himself because he couldn't really swim and one of the Eagle Scout tasks has to do with treading water for many hours in an icy lake in your blue uniform, or something like that. My father could doggy-paddle, but he couldn't risk putting his head underwater because of a Depression-era mastoid operation in his ear that had left a large hole. So, like my father, I never became an Eagle Scout. I never even went back to the minor leagues of the Boy Scouts—the Cub Scouts. That picnic ended my scouting career.

A few days after the picnic, and after several more episodes of painful, constricting back spasms, my mother took me to an orthopedist, who had unusually hairy fingers and a stern manner. He tapped me all over and massaged me roughly with his unattractive digits, seeking a diagnosis. I'm not sure he came up with one, but he prescribed that I wear a corset, saying that my back needed to be held in, and the way he said it made me feel as if I was being punished for some weakness of my character, rather than just a weakness in my lower back. And what an unusual, outdated prescription—how many other boys, I wonder, in 1972, were advised by physicians to be corseted?

So my mother, thinking that you always obey doctors, took me to a hospital pharmacy that had prosthetic devices and other gadgets—special toilet seats, harnesses, organ trusses—and I was fitted and measured for my corset by a small, bald pharmacist who used the same kind of measuring tape as a tailor.

My corset was white with silver buckles and had metal rods to keep my back from dissembling. I wore it for a year and was deeply humiliated. Only once did that corset give me any pleasure. I was with all the children on my street watching a Ping-Pong game in the garage of a neighbor. One of the players, an older boy, had perceived that I had interfered with one of his shots (this was untrue—he was losing badly and wanted someone to blame), and he started chasing me. I raced up my neighbor's driveway and across their lawn. I was wearing a heavy sweatshirt to cover the bulk of my corset, so my pursuer didn't know about my condition. He was right behind me, but even with the corset, I was able to scoot quickly. The other kids came running, too. The enraged boy was fat and had white-blond hair. He still held his paddle. He was going to try and smack me with it. He ran well despite his weight. Like in a dream, where you can't run, my legs did begin to feel heavy, and I felt the nausea that comes before the inevitable submission to a beating.

So when he caught up to me at the end of my neighbor's lawn, he hit me as hard as he could with his Ping-Pong paddle right in my lower back. It was going to be the first of several blows, but I didn't feel a thing and I heard a snapping of wood and I turned around just in time to see the circular part of the paddle fly in the air like a Frisbee and then land at the feet of the other children, our audience. The blond boy had unwittingly smashed his little racquet against my hidden metal rods, my secret armor, and it had severed the disclike head, which in a strange act of physics had ricocheted dramatically upward and, as I said, come down to earth at the feet of our amazed peers. So my attacker stood there holding the handle of his decapitated paddle, and he was stunned, defeated. Everyone laughed at him. It was a moment of triumph.

But that was the only victory my corset gave me, and in the middle of this time of wearing my corrective garment, I had another problem: My left testicle ascended and wouldn't come down. I was taken to another doctor and he told my mother that this wasn't uncommon in young boys and was usually a temporary condition. So luckily for me, he didn't recommend some kind of organ truss to pull the testicle down, which would have complimented my white waist-cincher, but the doctor did say that if my testicle didn't return home by the time I started puberty, then surgery might be necessary. And I was mature enough to know that surgery in the area of one's penis was not a desired event.

I'm not sure why my testicle went into hiding, but, like my back problem, I think it was fear-related: I found the third grade to be very stressful academically. There was an enormous quota of dittoes to be filled out each day, and three days a week, in the afternoons, I was starting to go to Hebrew school; so this overload of education had me quite nervous. My mother, a schoolteacher herself, expected me to be a perfect student, and I was terribly afraid that I couldn't be. In fact, I pleaded with her to let me drop out of everything (it was all too difficult; for the first few weeks of third grade I cried every night and pounded my feet into my bed), but she wouldn't let me quit—how could she?—and I started learning then that we spend most of our lives doing what we don't want to do. And so like a scared soldier in a bunker whose testicles are known to elevate during heavy shelling (to protect them, and then they descend during peacetime, which accounts for postwar baby booms), my testicle elevated during this fearful period of my life. Why only one went up, and not two, is a mild flaw in my theory, but let me press on.

So I was missing a testicle and wearing a corset. I was eight years old.

Then my health, on its own, improved. By the time I was nine and a half, all my problems cleared up. The testicle ended its strike and returned to work and the corset was banished to my underwear drawer, where it stayed for several years, a terrible sight, a terrible reminder.

I began to play a lot of sports, and I excelled at soccer and tennis. I was quite happy for almost two years. I had nothing to worry about. But then when I was eleven something unexpected occurred: My best friend started puberty. I saw him naked when we were changing to go swimming. I was shocked. His enlarged penis and thatch of pubic hair looked vulgar to my eyes, and yet I wanted the same thing to happen to me. I didn't say anything to him about his hairy penis; I pretended not to have noticed, but I was secretly hurt that he hadn't mentioned his transformation. It seemed like the kind of thing that a best friend should confide in you about. So I didn't really enjoy our afternoon swim, the whole thing had me feeling conflicted, and that evening, looking for parental counsel, I asked my mother when I would get hair and have a big penis.

"One day," she said, "some fluid, not urine, will come out of your penis. At night. And after that happens you'll get pubic hair and your penis will get bigger."

Some fluid. *Not urine.* This was very mysterious. I thought it must be a once-in-a-lifetime secretion that marked one's passage into adulthood, something akin to a caterpillar transforming into a butterfly, which was the scientific equivalent I came up with—back then one was always seeing in school slow-motion films of such metamorphoses. So I was naive and unusually innocent; I never figured out until well after the fact that my mother had been referring to a wet dream.

Thus, I waited for this unknown, unnamed fluid for the next four and a half years, while all the girls and boys around me began to change and grow. As a result, I developed an acute awareness and fascination for that surest and most visible sign of puberty—armpit hair. I was always noting with sad jealousy the armpit hairs of my peers in the gym locker room; and I was forever inspecting my own armpits in the mirror at home. I'd shine a flashlight on them, hoping to spot the most meager follicle. But my pits were barren; no hairs flourished. Then one time on the school bus, in the spring of sixth grade, I saw a *girl's* lovely blond armpit hairs when she grabbed hold of the pole near the driver. I was mesmerized, enchanted. My little penis turned immediately to stone. This girl was becoming a woman before my eyes—*she had hair!* Beautiful, gold-blond armpit hair. It was glorious. I desired her and I envied her and I never forgot her. Fourteen years later, while visiting the Greek island of Santorini, I saw an attractive German woman's blond armpit hair and I was transported back in time—like Proust with his madeleine—to that vision of blond armpit hair on the school bus, and my reaction in Greece, all those years later, was exactly the same: I was enchanted and my penis turned to stone.

One summer during my teenage years, when I was waiting for my Godotish puberty, I went away to a Jewish Camp in Upstate New York. I was in the Levi division (Levi was the name of one of the original Hebrew tribes before it became a pair of jeans) of newly christened teenagers, and to my horror I discovered that I was the only boy who still had a small, undeveloped penis and no pubic hair! So I had to hide myself the whole summer. I would quickly change my clothes with my back to my tentmates, and I only showered early in the morning when no one else was around. It was nerve-racking. But one person did see my naked form—the head counselor of Levi, who was the best-looking counselor in the whole camp with his curly blond hair and perfect physique, and who decided one night that he should assist me in putting calamine lotion on my body for a very bad case of poison ivy I had contracted. To do this, he took me up to the shower room when no one was there. He had me strip down to my underwear and he began to coat me with the pink lotion. Then he inquired as to whether or not I had the rash in my groin area. I admitted that I did, so he knelt in front of me and began to pull down my underwear. I was extremely embarrassed and before my secret, tiny penis was revealed, I made an apology—I whispered, "I'm very small."

I wasn't worried about being sexually abused; it was the 1970s and sexual abuse hadn't been invented yet. I was simply concerned about someone finding out that I hadn't started puberty. So down came my underwear and the counselor put the lotion on my small penis, and he said, "Don't worry, you have plenty of time." This was very sweet and kind of him, though I felt a little funny when he quickly pulled up my underwear when he heard the door to the shower room open up. I intuited that what had occurred was perhaps not proper. And sure enough, this very nice, handsome counselor left the camp several years later under ominous circumstances. I still do wonder what became of him. For me, my encounter with him was actually quite tender. Before the judge, if I was ever called, I would say, "He was very reassuring."

And that counselor was right. I did have plenty of time. I turned fourteen, then fifteen, but still no armpit hair or fluid. I was starting to lose my mind over this. Then in the spring of my freshman year of high school, this puberty situation got really out of control when I made the tennis team. It was late March when I was selected for the squad—it was an honor to have been chosen as a freshman—and because it was still cold out, our practices were held at an indoor racquet club before school started. At the end of the first practice, our coach, who was short and dark and bore a slight resemblance to my father, announced that every day after we were done playing we were to go for a jog around the parking lot and then come in and shower. Showering was mandatory, he said, because we couldn't go to school smelling of sweat. "It's not healthy," he explained.

I didn't know how I was going to escape exposure and humiliation. I hadn't been seen naked for years, except by the understanding counselor at camp. I was practically of normal height for my age, but that was the only normal thing about me. My lack of puberty was my most guarded secret. I regretted having tried out for the team. I hadn't considered the showering. There had been no showering during try-outs, and in the fall when I was on the freshman soccer team, none of us had showered.

I thought my only chance, after we finished that first practice, was to be the fastest runner. So when we took off for our jog, I dashed ahead of the pack, raced around the lot, sped into the locker room, stripped down to my underwear, and headed for the showers. But before I could get anywhere, some of the other boys, who had also run fast, began to straggle in. It was impossible to go through with it. The shower area didn't have private booths; it was just a large tiled room with spigots coming out of the walls.

I sat down on the bench and began to dress. I watched enviously as the other boys marched around carefree with their large penises. They took towels out of the towel bin and didn't even bother to put them around their waists. Each boy's penis and surrounding pubic hair seemed to be as distinctive as his face and hairdo. Some of the boys were eighteen years old—they were practically men. It was unfair. I was a cherub compared to them. My penis was indistinguishable from that of a five-year-old's. I could still do the trick of pushing it in so that it disappeared momentarily, went to Connecticut or someplace and then came back to me in New Jersey.

So that first day, I didn't shower. I got dressed and headed out of the locker room just as the coach was coming in. He looked at me accusingly and said, "Showered already?" I lied immediately. "Yes, Coach," I said, and he let it pass, though I knew he was suspicious.

I was nerve-racked for the next twenty-four hours, and at the end of the second practice, I again sprinted ahead of everyone in our tour of the parking lot, running even faster than the day before, and my teammates all thought I was trying to be the coach's pet. But I was running for my life. A sophomore on the team tried to keep up with me, the bastard, but I left him behind. I made it to the locker room and had about a minute to take a shower. I got down to my underwear but could go no further. I was too afraid. Then a few of my teammates came in. I tried to summon the courage to reveal myself, but I couldn't. So I sat on the bench and got dressed and I felt surrounded by the hairy penises of my team-mates; it was dizzying, things felt out of focus, all those penises, it was like being in Hitchcock's *The Birds*.

I staggered out to the lobby to wait for a ride to school from one of the hairy seniors. As I stood there the coach came up to me. He looked at my hair and said, "You didn't shower, did you?" It was incredible; it was only the second day of practice and he was already honing in on the most vulnerable aspect of my life.

"I don't want to get a wet head," I said. "I have a little cold, and if I go out with a wet head, it might get worse. I washed a little in the sink." I was always being warned by my great-aunt Pearl, who often stayed with my family, about the dangers of a wet head, that a wet head could lead to serious illness.

"All right," the coach said, "but tomorrow you better shower."

Why did he care? Why couldn't he leave me alone? The next day after practice I just sat on the locker-room bench in my underwear, my barrier to humiliation, and I was practically catatonic with indecision. Should I just do it? Let them see me and laugh at me? Then the coach came and stood before me. He was nude. A towel was draped over his shoulder. His penis looked like a purple old man hiding in a black marsh. It looked like a poisonous mushroom, a chanterelle from hell. It looked like my father's penis. My father's penis, which I was always seeing in the bathroom and I would try not to look at it, but it would look at me no matter where I was, like the Mona Lisa.

But the coach, despite his unattractive penis, wasn't a bad man and he had an inkling of the problem I was having. He may have even thought he was helping me, as my coach, to conquer something. He probably figured I was only suffering from shyness. If he had known how small I was, he might have left me alone.

"So you're going to take a shower," he said cheerfully, yet forcefully, trying to manipulate me. "There's nothing to be worried about. It's healthy to take a shower after exercising. But you better hurry up, you're running late."

He walked off to the tiled room, sure that I would follow him. I regarded his unbecoming lower-back hair, and then dressed as fast as I could and escaped out to the lobby to the pay phone. I called my mother in a panic to come save me. I was almost crying. I said, "Mom, come get me right away. Please!" Luckily, she hadn't left early to go teach at her high school, and I begged her to meet me at the gas station, which was down the street from the tennis club. I didn't want the coach to find me.

When she pulled up in her car, I felt tremendous love for her. We were very close back then and always had been. I was an immature boy, not just physically, and my mother had encouraged this. Behind my father's back she had continued buying me G.I. Joe dolls, though by the time I was fifteen I would only play with them in my closet so that my father couldn't see me. I would have them hold on to the hangers with their special gripping hands, and when I wasn't playing with them, I just liked seeing them hiding in the closet when I would get dressed in the morning. I felt less alone and I must have identified with them—they were masculine but had no genitals.

So my father didn't know about the G.I. Joes, but he was quite aware of my close relationship with my mother. Long before I knew what it meant, he often called me Oedipus. He would summon me to the dinner table by shouting, "Oedipus! Oedipus!" He also said it whenever he saw my mother giving me a kiss. And when that would happen, my sister, three years older than me, would join my father in calling me Oedipus, and she would also make a heart shape with her hands.

My father's other frequent nickname for me was Dick Tracy because of my large, bent nose. My penis was small but my nose was big. So there was a certain parallel to my father's nicknames for me: Oedipus and Dick Tracy—two mystery-solvers.

And my father was right. It was all very Oedipal. For years my mother and I had played this game where she would ask, "Who loves you?" It became a game because she asked me so often. I'd answer by naming one of my grandparents or my father or my sister. Then she'd ask again, "Who loves you?" and I'd name another person, but she'd keep asking, "Who loves you?" And the more relatives or friends of the family that I could think of, the more suspenseful it became. But then finally I'd always submit and shout, "You do!" And this shout not only affirmed that she loved me, but that I was crazy about her. And when I was with my mother in that car, being saved from my tennis coach and my teammates, I loved her very much. I told her what was going on.

"The other boys won't notice," she said.

"They'll notice! I'm the only one who hasn't started puberty. They'll kill me!"

My mother wanted me to talk to my father, but I wouldn't do that. I hadn't let him see me naked for a long time. I must have sensed intuitively the other side of the Oedipal dynamic—that if my father knew I wasn't a threat, i.e., a mature male, he could easily do away with me. He was a member of the NRA.

So I wanted to quit the tennis team immediately, but my mother wouldn't let me. Still, she was sweet to me; she reassured me that someday soon I would develop. You have plenty of time, she said. I had heard it before, but I was running out of time—I needed to start puberty by the next practice.

It didn't happen. The next day, the coach was going from court to court observing us. I was on line for a backhand drill and he stood next to me and said in a snide way, "Think you'll shower today?" I didn't say anything to him. I was too embarrassed, and he walked away from me. And then a few minutes later during a volley drill, as I made my approach to the net, I fainted. I remember seeing the net cord and rotating my hand for the proper grip on the racquet, and then there was the cement of the court rising up to slap me, but there was also the feeling of relief, of going to sleep. I'm sure the coach, for a moment, saw an opening as I lay passed out. "Let's strip down Ames and see what he's got!"

But he restrained himself and my mother was called and I was taken to a doctor. I had mononucleosis. I had never kissed a girl, I was still in love with my G.I. Joes, and yet I had come down with the kissing disease. I must have picked it up from a water fountain or an improperly washed utensil in the cafeteria, or a wet head had done the trick. In any event, it was the best thing that could have happened to me—I missed the rest of the tennis season, and I never played competitively again.

That summer, a few months removed from my trauma on the tennis team, I began to experiment instinctively with masturbation. I still hadn't started puberty, but each night I strummed myself for a few minutes before falling asleep. I found it soothing, and I say *strum,* because I've never been one to jerk on my penis, unlike most men, who employ that rapid up-and-down yanking, which when I've witnessed other men masturbating—in parks or public rest rooms, those sorts of locales—I've always found to be somewhat violent and unattractive.

Anyway, one night as I strummed in the motion and rhythm peculiar to me, my penis seemed larger than it ever had been before, and then a dribble of clear substance came out with a noticeably pleasurable feeling. I had heard about orgasms by this time, but it was only at that moment that I made the connection between "coming" and the fluid I had been waiting so long for (which I had just about given up on). I immediately went running to my mother.

My father was out of town, which he often was as a salesman, and my sister had already left home, on her long journey to becoming a psychiatrist, having sensed early on, I imagine, what was going on in the old Oedipal household. So it was around ten o'clock at night and I sprinted down the hall to my parents' bedroom completely nude. I burst in upon my mother, who was propped up in bed reading. I shouted at her with joy, "Mom, it's happened! The fluid came out! I think I'm starting puberty! My penis seems bigger!"

I got onto the bed next to her. She didn't say a thing to me. She kept on reading her book, she wouldn't look at me, but I could see that she was smiling. I figured that she was happy for me. I knew that I was happy. In fact, I was delirious, which seems to be the only explanation for my unusual behavior. In my delirious, exuberant state it felt perfectly natural to share this with my mother, who looked beautiful and kind sitting there. Her long blond hair, normally fastened in a bun, was loose and lay over her shoulders. I felt like snuggling next to her. In my mind, she had been waiting four and a half years with me for my pubescence, ever since I first asked her when I would change. She had been my sole confidante. She was the only person who knew my secret about how tiny I was, and she was the only one who knew what I had gone through on the tennis team.

And as I lay beside her on the bed, I admired my penis. I felt like all my problems were over. I decided to masturbate again. I wanted to show her how I could do it. "Watch, Mom," I said. "It gets big." I wanted to impress her. She was still smiling, but still not looking at me, which I thought was strange—she was always attentive to my accomplishments. And then when I touched myself, she said, "Maybe you should do that in your room."

She didn't say it with disgust or anger, her tone was gentle, but suddenly I felt shame. I knew then that it wasn't normal to show your mother your first official erection. I slid off her bed and I ran to her bedroom door, cupping my penis in my hands, holding myself like Adam, guilty with knowledge. I scurried down the hall, wondering if she might tell my father. I was embarrassed, but I also wanted to try masturbating again. I had started puberty! My troubles were over. New ones were beginning, but I didn't know it yet. I opened the door to my room. I was leaving my mother behind, and she may have sensed this, felt the umbilical-Oedipal cord snapping, and she tried to bring me back. She played our game, but it was too late. She'd had her chance. She called out, "Who loves you?"

Hair Piece

IN JANUARY OF 1995, during a fit of depression, while living at home with my parents in New Jersey, I took my father's tiny electric beard trimmer and shaved my head. Because of the trimmer's size and the dullness of its single blade, the whole scalping process took almost forty minutes. This would seem to be the act of a rebellious teenager, but at the time I was thirty-one years old.

I was depressed for a number of reasons (I was broke and in debt and living at home, after all), but one of the chief causes of my depression, before I attacked my hair, was that I was going bald in a very strange manner. I had hair on the sides, on the point, on the back, and I had a hairline in place on my forehead, but behind the hairline was a large bald spot. I didn't have my bald spot in the back of my head, but at the front! I combed the hairline, which I called the hedge or the fringe, back over this spot, but you could see right through the hedge/fringe to the empty lot behind, and if a strong wind came along, the fringe/hedge was knocked over and my spot was exposed. (Please see diagram/map on the next page, and author photograph on cover.)

I'd always had a nice head of hair, but as my hair thinned, I felt that I was sallying forth into the world with a faulty helmet. I was

MY HAIR

LEGEND

Fringe: ((((((((

Strong: xxxxxx

Weak: ₀₀₀₀₀₀

Very Weak: ⋯⋯⋯

defenseless, vulnerable, laughable. A friend of mine suggested that I had mange. It was all too much. At the nadir, I wrote in my journal: "I feel very bad today and very bald." So then I shaved my whole head to match the bald spot.

The result was disastrous. I am pale and have white eyebrows, and so by shaving my hair and removing all color from my visage, the effect was as if I had erased my head. I was now an invisible man.

This wasn't too bad because I started commuting to New York to teach grammar at a business college, and since the students hated the subject, it was good that I was invisible. All they could see was a jacket and tie that had a voice emanating from the neck hole. I maintained my invisible-man status by shaving my head weekly with a pair of barber's clippers.

The grammar job was my ticket out of my parents' house in New Jersey and I moved to Brooklyn. On my own again, my depression lifted and after a few months, I decided to regrow my hair. I'd often had dreams that my hair was back, looking lustrous and beautiful, and I missed it terribly, like an amputee dreaming of a limb.

Unfortunately, my hair looked terrible as it came in. The hedge/fringe wasn't long enough yet to comb back over the bald spot, so I looked like I had a monk's tonsure, except that it was at the front of my head.

During this time of painful regrowth, the late spring of '95, I was doing research into WASP culture and had managed to get invited to a grand party at a Newport mansion. I put on my blue blazer and drove up to Rhode Island. I was having a good time at the party, but then a drunk older gentleman, a white-haired yachtsman, asked me a question, and he was quite sincere and concerned. "Have you had brain surgery?" he asked.

"My God, no," I said. "Why do you ask?"

"Oh, I'm sorry," he said. "I thought you had an operation in that SPOT." And he pointed his swollen, ancient mariner's finger right at my prow, my forward-placed tonsure.

The next day, I reshaved my head and it stayed that way for two years. Then this July (1997), I moved from Brooklyn to the East Village and I couldn't stand seeing how many men had shaved heads. I didn't want to be a soldier in a trendy, bald army, so I decided to be brave and regrow my hair.

I wore a hat all through July, and then in mid-August I saw an ad in my very own paper, *New York Press,* that intrigued me. Hair Club for Men wanted men with thinning hair to send in photos. If they chose you for a commercial, the reward was five hundred dollars. I needed the money, and so my father took several pictures of my head from different angles and I mailed them in. I also included a cover letter, stating that I thought I would make an excellent poster boy for balding.

Several weeks went by and I didn't hear from them and I forgot about the whole thing. In the meantime, I was busy regrowing my hair. I had done some research on the subject and I was taking certain actions. I was trying to quit coffee since it robbed my body of hair-related vitamins, and I was avoiding masturbation because I read a book on Eastern practices of semen-retention, which told me that masturbation dried up my spinal fluid and made my hair fall out. I've now come to see my bald spot and the bald spots of other men as the mark of Cain for excessive self-abuse.

I also purchased rosemary oil, which is very good for scalp health, and a rubber scalp invigorator. And I started eating lots of sea vegetables because I read that people in Asian cultures had very good hair and that their diet was rich in seaweed.

So now every time I relapse on coffee or masturbation, which I do with appalling frequency—coffee is so difficult to give up—I quickly run into the kitchen and fetch from the cupboard some seaweed. Most convenient, in a vacuum-sealed bag, is dried dulse, which is salty and tough, but I eat it to apologize to my hair and to try to convince it not to fall out. It's a mad game of tug-of-war (sea vegetables vs. onanism and caffeine), but I think the seaweed is winning—my hair looks pretty good.

Then the other day, I was poring over my enormous credit-card bills and I remembered the photos I had sent to Hair Club for Men. I called them up to find out what was going on. I needed that five hundred dollars. I spoke to several operators, and then I was put right through to Shari Sperling, the daughter of Sy Sperling, the founder of the company. I was excited to have made it to the top, and she was wonderfully friendly and vivacious over the phone. I asked about my pictures, she said she remembered them, and I asked if I was in the running for the commercial. I also mentioned that I was a writer for the *New York Press,* hoping that she would take me more seriously. After all, I wasn't just another desperate man with thinning hair—I was a *journalist* with thinning hair.

"Did you write an article about having crabs and venereal diseases?" she asked, referring to my essay in the *Press,* "A *W* on My *P.*"

I wasn't counting on her actually having read me, so I wasn't sure if her familiarity with my work was good *or* bad for my credibility. But I pretended that it was good. "Yes, that crab-piece was some of my best work," I said.

"I love your stuff," she said.

"Well, thank you," I said, flattered, but then I pressed on with the more important issue at hand. "So what do you think of my pictures? Can you use me?"

She said that my hair was too short for what they were looking for. I told her that it had grown in some and that my fringe certainly would be a good selling point, that other men with fringe problems would identify, which I thought was a compelling argument and sure to get me in position for that much-needed five hundred dollars.

"I know that fringe thing can be bad," she said sympathetically. "We had one guy in here with a fringe and it looked like armpit hair at the front of his head. That's why I feel good about what we do for people. We make them look better, feel better."

I took some offense at this armpit remark, but I didn't let on. I tried to convince her to use me for the commercial, but it was to no avail, though she was very sweet about it. So since I had her on the phone, I asked her how Hair Club for Men did what it did. For years, I had seen the ads where they stated with pride that they used *real* hair. I had always wondered where they got this hair. I figured that they took it from your chest or your legs or the back of your head or, even better, your lower back, which is such an unattractive place to have hair—I even repulse myself when I scratch that area and find my little nest of down in that unusual spot. I feel terrible for the poor women who have to grasp me there during our sexual congresses. Anyway, I wasn't sure where exactly Hair Club got its hair. So I asked, "Where do you get that *real* hair? From the back of the man's head?"

"Asia," she said.

"What do you mean Asia?"

"People sell their hair over there. It's the strongest hair in the world. We deal with hair brokers."

"That's interesting. I've read that people in Asia have good hair, but it's a bit strange that they sell it."

"Don't think it's just an Asian thing," she said, worried perhaps that I was going to accuse her of Third World cheap-labor exploitation. "American women sell their hair to wig-makers all the time." This last statement produced in me a vision of attractive Midwestern women going around with closely cropped heads. I thought of the Midwest, I guess, because that to me is America, and Shari Sperling had said *American women.*

"What do you do with the hair once you get it?" I asked.

"We dye it and put it through processes to change the texture and then it's attached to your own hair with a nontoxic skin-compatible fusion. A fringe is good to have, by the way, if you become a client, because you can attach hair to it."

"I'm glad my fringe is good for something," I said, though I had no intention of joining the Club since they didn't want to use me in their ad campaign. Shortly thereafter we rang off and I was a little disturbed by the thought of poor people in Asia continually growing and shaving off their hair. But then I realized it was not unlike what I had been doing for the last few years. And at least they were getting paid for it, and it was probably a good part-time seasonal job—grow it in the winter, shave it in the summer. It was practically agricultural.

Then I thought how I was doing all the right things for my hair: I was living like the people of Asia—I was retaining my semen (well, at least making an effort) and I was eating sea vegetables. Then it occurred to me that if I moved to Asia, I might get *all* my hair back. The total cure for balding was to live in the Orient. I could support myself by teaching grammar again. And then when my hair was the strongest in the world, I could have my revenge for not being used in the commercial. I'd shave off my beautiful hair and sell it to Hair Club for Men, and I'd get a lot more than the five hundred dollars I had originally been hoping for.

The Playboys of Northern New Jersey

M Y FIRST SEXUAL EXPERIENCE with a woman was rather old-fashioned: It was with a prostitute. I was sixteen years old and I was living where I had always lived—in the tranquil and dead and middle-class suburbs of northern New Jersey. It was February of 1981 and a friend of mine, who was seventeen and thus had a driver's license, was working for a florist as a deliveryman. For some reason, his last delivery on this particular Saturday night was all the way to Brooklyn—to a funeral home. He called me up and suggested that I come with him. After we dropped off the flowers, we could go to Manhattan and drink; he had the store's station wagon and his bosses would never know what time he brought it back.

I hesitated. Brooklyn, in my mind, was very far away and was where Jews, like my parents, used to live before fleeing for New Jersey or Long Island—so who would ever go back to Brooklyn? It must be a dangerous place now, I thought; a place that if there was such a thing as a Jewish tourist map would be circled in red, and a red circle in the map's legend would mean: *There Used to Be Beautiful Jewish Neighborhoods Here*—which was a sad refrain I had heard all my childhood while being driven through such environs as Paterson, upper Manhattan, the Bronx, and, of course, Brooklyn.

"Don't be a wimp," said my friend over the phone. His name was Werner.

I didn't want him to think I was a coward, so I said, "All right, I'll go," and he came to pick me up. My parents were out of town—I could come home as late as I wanted.

I had known Werner for a very long time. He was always tall and thin for his age; his drawn-in cheeks gave him a malnourished appearance, but he was good-looking nonetheless, with blue eyes and sandy blond hair. I considered him to be a good friend but not a great friend. Our association seemed to peak around the first grade, and after that our closeness was sporadic. My parents, though, were always proud of my friendship with Werner. They saw it as a sign of their liberalness and capacity for forgiveness that they let me play with a boy of such obvious German descent—Werner's father had been an innocent, teenaged foot soldier in the Third Reich, but was a very nice man. And I think Werner's parents saw it as a sign of their assimilation that their son should have a little Jewish friend. So everyone was happy.

At the height of our friendship, in the first grade, Werner and I played this game one time that we called the Playboy Club. Neither of us had ever seen a *Playboy* magazine, but we had heard from Werner's older brother, who was in middle school, about this club where men drank and had the most amazing experiences. These experiences weren't elaborated on by Werner's brother, but we perceived that they were *sexy*. We weren't entirely sure what *sexy* meant, but it was an exciting word. So Werner and I went down into his family's paneled basement and sat at his father's bar. We poured Coca-Cola into shot glasses and we ate pretzels and listened to the radio. We thought we were doing everything that one should do in a Playboy Club and we waited for something *sexy* to happen.

So we sat there for some time, waiting, and I remember thinking that the game was rather disappointing. And Werner didn't say anything, but I knew he was thinking the same thing, but we both didn't want to admit that we had come up with a bad game and that we didn't know why, that we didn't know what was missing. When we finally gave up and got down from the bar, we engaged in some seven-year-old wrestling and rolling on top of one another to relieve our frustrations, though it was unclear to us why we were frustrated.

Then almost ten years later, we were still frustrated, but now we had more of an idea why, and that's how we came to be driving across the Brooklyn Bridge together, hoping to find a funeral home in Bay Ridge. We wanted alcohol, but behind the desire to drink was the desire for sex, love, a kiss. I was completely inexperienced with girls, Werner a little less so, but we had both heard and were learning that the way to meet women was through drinking.

So as we drove through Brooklyn, I thought for sure we would get lost, but Werner, being German and capable, was able to read the map and locate the final resting place of our flowers' recipient. It was a small Italian funeral home with a low ceiling, and there was a bald man in a black suit sitting by the closed, shiny coffin. It was cold inside the home; it was a freezing February night, and the man had an ancient, orange-glowing electric heater for company. He appeared to be some kind of professional coffin-guarder (he didn't even have a newspaper), and he took the flowers from Werner and put them with several other bouquets by some stacked chairs in the corner.

Our morose delivery accomplished, we were eager for our adventure and Werner navigated us back to Manhattan, where we asked somebody on the street how to get to Greenwich Village. We figured that's where the good drinking was. We made our way to Thompson Street and West Third and went to a bar called Googie's, which I believe still exists. Inside was a hardy crowd seeking the warmth of company and alcohol, and luckily for us, the bartender didn't ask for any proof of age.

Werner almost did expose our youth, though, by ordering a pitcher of Alabama Slammers, but we got away with it. We sat at a little table and the drink was a grotesque, red-colored, sweet-tasting concoction, and I became completely intoxicated. We thought of approaching two single women, but we lacked courage.

Then midway through our second pitcher, I stood up to proclaim something and I knocked over our table and I fell down and the pitcher came down with me and made a blood-colored pool on the floor. "I've been wounded," I shouted. I was hoisted up by the back of my coat and thrown out the door by the bartender, just like in the movies. Werner followed after me, laughing, and we weaved in the cold to the car.

For some reason, I didn't vomit. We did jumping jacks to sober up and then we drove off. We tried to find the Lincoln Tunnel, and as we came down a street, in the Thirties, near Tenth Avenue, we saw, like a hallucination, about half a dozen women standing on a street corner. Steam came out of their painted mouths and they were in miniskirts and stockings and fur coats. They beckoned to us and smiled. They wanted us.

"Oh, my God, whores," said Werner, excited.

"They look sexy," I said.

He pulled the floral wagon to the side of the road and rolled down his window. He entered into rapid negotiations with a dyed blonde—"A blowjob is ten dollars, sweetie," she said, "Okay," he said, "Pull into that lot," she said, pointing, "Okay," he said—and he backed up a hundred feet and then turned into this abandoned lot. He drove into the dark, far corner and we turned around and watched the whore come to us on her high heels, like a woman on stilts, it seemed. As she got close to the car, he said, "Get out."

"Can't I sit in the back?" I asked. It wasn't that I wanted to watch, but I was a little scared to stand in a dark lot in the freezing cold.

"Don't be fucking crazy," he said, and then he softened his tone. "You can go after me."

"I don't want to," I said, with some disgust. I was taking the moral upper hand because it wasn't pleasing to my ego to be second, but more important, I was covering up my fear. I was intimidated—I had never kissed a girl, so I was hardly ready for a blowjob.

I got out of the car and held the door open for the blonde. "Thank you," she said. She had nice manners.

I went and stood next to an old metal trailer—a truck with a body but no head. I thought I would be safe in its shadows, and it all felt romantically dangerous since I was still quite drunk. I shivered in the cold and I leaned against the truck and tried to see what was happening in the station wagon, which was about ten yards away, but there wasn't much to see, only Werner's hands on the steering wheel, his thin face staring straight ahead, looking at nothing. The blonde had disappeared. Then I glanced to the street corner and saw that a big black woman was approaching me. She was all hips and red lips.

"You want a blowjob, baby?"

"Okay," I said quietly. One doesn't think to say no in these situations—at least I don't.

"You have ten dollars?"

"Yes."

"You pay before we play." I took out my wallet. I had exactly ten dollars left. It seemed like kismet.

I handed her the money and she put it in her purse. Then she squatted down in front of me like a baseball catcher. She had me open up my winter coat so that she could get at my fly. She took out my penis and it was rather small because of the freezing temperatures, and because I was afraid—she was the first woman besides my mother and sister who had ever seen my penis.

"I'm kind of cold," I said, explaining my small stature.

"That's all right, I'm gonna warm you up," she said, and then she put her mouth on it. Oh, Lord, I loved it. No one had ever touched me so nicely. I closed my eyes.

Prostitutes didn't use condoms back then, and I responded to the warmth and heat of her mouth, and I came rather quickly. I opened my eyes and she stood up.

"Okay, baby," she said, and she turned and walked away, done with me.

I felt giddy and happy. Doubly drunk. Drunk now on sex, on life. "Thank you," I said, calling after her, and then I added, since I was smitten and drunk, "I like you." And it was true. I did like her. I felt even that I loved her. And I thought she must like me after doing what she did. But she didn't turn around. She kept walking. I figured she couldn't hear me. Then the car door slammed. Werner's blonde walked across the lot. I ran over to the station wagon.

"I got a blowjob," I said with pride.

"Me too," said Werner, but he was quiet, sullen, hurt by it somehow.

He raced backward out of the lot and onto the street. I looked for my new girlfriend with the others on the corner. Then we pulled up to the corner, stopped by the red light. I saw her; she was drinking tea out of a Styrofoam cup. Several of them were drinking tea—I could see the strings of the tea bags, the steam coming off the tops of the cups.

I was happy to spot her. I rolled down my window. She looked at me. I waved to her and she approached the car.

"I don't think you heard me before," I said. "I really like you." I was innocent, stupid, a fool. What did I hope for by saying such a thing? But I wanted to express my affection. I was sixteen and had never kissed a girl.

She threw her tea in my face and turned her back to me. The other whores laughed. Werner laughed, too. The tea wasn't scalding, just hot. The light changed and we drove off. I didn't say anything. Werner held in the rest of his laughter. I dried my face with my shirt. I regretted my ten dollars. We found the tunnel.

I didn't know if she thought I was taunting her or if she was simply teaching me what I needed to learn. And I didn't know if they drank tea to stay warm or to wash the taste of sperm out of their mouths.

An Erection Is a Felony

I HEARD ABOUT THE ARTIST and fellow pervert Harry Chandler before I ever met him. It was the spring of 1995, and I was in bed with a girl I was dating, and I was telling her parts of my life story. I regaled her with the trauma of my late puberty, recounting how it didn't arrive until I was fifteen and a half.

"That's nothing," she said. "My last boyfriend didn't start puberty until he was twenty-one."

"My God," I said. I thought of how I nearly went insane waiting for pubic hair, but at least I got it by the time I was a sophomore in high school. This poor fellow would have nearly been a senior in college. "How old is he now?" I asked.

"Thirty-seven."

"Is he still severely affected by his late puberty?"

"He's pretty crazy. But I don't think it's the puberty issue. He lost a foot eight years ago. I think that made him crazy. He thinks he has all these allergies because he lost the foot. He doesn't eat wheat or sugar, and he didn't like it when I ate sugar. He said it made me pasty-looking and puffy. Can you believe that?"

I glanced over at her in the moonlight that was coming through her bedroom window. She *did* look pasty and puffy. I was also against wheat and sugar. She didn't know this yet about me; we'd only been going out for a month. I felt a secret kinship with her ex-boyfriend.

"Was it strange to be in bed with someone who was missing a foot?"

"It wasn't too weird. It's like he has a pole from the knee down. It's phallic. I got kind of crazy one time and I took off his prosthesis and I had him touch me with his stump, but it didn't really work out."

"What's your ex-boyfriend's name?"

"Harry Chandler. But he's not related to Raymond Chandler, in case you're wondering. Everyone always asks that."

The girl and I broke up a few weeks later. That was two years ago, and New York being a small town, I met Harry Chandler a few times and there was always this feeling that we desperately needed to talk to each other, but every time we crossed paths, we were in crowded social situations. Only once did we have a conversation of any length. We were at a birthday party and we spoke for ten minutes and for some reason we exchanged stories of being raped by dogs. As a boy, Harry had been pinned down by a Samoan husky who rubbed his exposed penis on Harry's face, and I told Harry about being pinned by an English sheepdog when I was a boy, and how the dog bit my neck and rubbed his wet, pink penis between my bare thighs. I was only wearing shorts. My sister had laughed and watched my rape, and then my uncle came and yanked the dog off me.

But it was only recently that Harry Chandler and I finally sat down and talked the way we needed to. He invited me to come sit with him in SoHo while he tried to sell his paintings.

"It's not bad," he said to me over the phone. "You just sit there and wait and hope that some tourist will want one. . . . It's a lot like fishing."

So on an unbearably hot July Saturday I went and found Harry Chandler at his regular fishing spot on the east side of West Broadway, just south of Spring Street. He had a table with three watercolor paintings, a chair, a sun umbrella, and two large oil paintings, about five feet high with temporary wooden supports. The watercolors were beach scenes Chandler had done while on Fire Island. They were light and beautiful, aimed at the summer tourists. The oils were city scenes, eerie and imbalanced portraits of New Yorkers and the street.

We sat on concrete stairs across from his work. Tourists streamed by, some of them pausing briefly to glance at the paintings. The sun was beating down on us, and I was wearing a baseball hat to protect my bald spot from skin cancer, and Chandler was wearing an old white bandanna. He is deeply tanned; he teaches art to children during the week on Fire Island and comes to SoHo for the weekends. His dark brown color and the tautness of his skin give him the look of a 1930s hobo, the kind of good-looking man who was set adrift in the Dust Bowl by the Depression.

He is thirty-nine years old, about five-foot-eleven, and he has high cheekbones, a clear brow, a beautiful nose, green eyes, and short, cropped blond hair. He is handsome, but there is also a terrible privation in his face; he's gaunt, and his crowded teeth are stained from tobacco, and there's a sad humility in his eyes that I've only seen in old bums on the Bowery, a humility born of self-inflicted pain and defeat. But he is quick to laugh at himself, his face can be loony and hopeful, so in some moments Chandler looks like he's in his twenties, and in other moments he could pass for a man in his late fifties.

So we sat there on West Broadway and I admired Chandler's face, but I was uncomfortable on the concrete stairs. I had developed a hemorrhoid recently and the hard, flat surface was putting pressure on it. I mentioned this to Chandler.

"Do you drink coffee?" he asked.

"I do, but I'm trying to quit. It's not good for hair."

"You *have* to give it up. I had a hemorrhoid once and I stopped coffee and it went away immediately."

"I'm afraid to give up coffee, even though I want to," I said.

"I'm afraid to drink it," he said. "I get too sexual. Can't really control myself. Makes me a little insane, I think. . . . When did you get this hemorrhoid?"

"A few weeks ago."

"You must be all tensed up inside. You should try this kava kava herb. It's like Prozac. It'll calm you down, help you sleep. But it might not work if you have coffee in your system. . . . I'm on a lot of herbs now. It's wonderful. I feel great. My brother is a homeo-pathic doctor and he's prescribed everything. I did it because my kidneys weren't working, and if you have a major organ in crisis, your whole system is affected. It can make you feel insane."

Once in a while a tourist paused for more than a second to stare at the paintings, and Chandler would get to his feet and hobble over to them and would say to them kindly, "I'm here if you have any questions."

But there were very few questions; the fish weren't biting. We talked about his career. He's been selling paintings on the streets of SoHo for the better part of four years. He's out there, sometimes seven days a week, from April to October, and he estimates that he has sold about two hundred paintings. That's not a bad rate of suc-cess, and a lot better than most working artists. He just about makes enough to pay his rent, buy food, and buy paints.

"I like the idea of fresh-air painting better than street artist," he said. "That's what the French call it, fresh air. There's nothing better than painting from life. That's what Van Gogh, Matisse, Gauguin, and Cézanne all did, painted from life. And being on the street to sell"—he gestured to West Broadway—"I think of this as my gallery. Every day is an exhibition, a show. . . . But it's also a curse to be out here. You get black-listed. They think if you're desperate enough to do this, then something's wrong with you. They label you as a street artist and they don't take you seriously. No gallery will look at my slides. . . . There is this one guy who might want to bring me indoors; he came by and gave me his card the other day, told me to call. He used to own a gallery. He's got one in Westchester now. But I'd still paint outside, I'd just rather not have to *sell* outside. It eats away at you. One time, I set up in front of this gallery, and this woman came out, turns out she was the owner, and she said, 'No peddlers.' 'I'm not a peddler,' I said, 'I'm an artist.' 'You're peddling your paintings,' she said. 'I'm *painting* my paintings,' I said. 'I don't care, I want you out of here,' she said. I crossed the street. It was humiliating. . . . But I've never been arrested for being out here. The cops sense that I am a sincere artist.

"One time, though, they did make me leave. I had just set up— twenty paintings. Had taken me an hour to get here, rolling my cart real slow. Then I had to pack everything back up. So then I was rolling the cart home and it tipped over on Canal Street. The light changed. Cars almost ran over my paintings. They were trying to get to the Holland Tunnel. Tears were streaming down my face, the failure of it. . . . But I'm used to crying in the street. Every couple of years the foot on my prosthesis just snaps off and I have to hop on one leg to a cab. I cry every time. It's upsetting when a part of your body snaps off."

Chandler was wearing light cotton pants and I looked at his left leg. There was a swelling under the material where the prosthesis is attached to the knee. But if you didn't know about it, you would never notice. And he was wearing sneakers on both feet, the real one and the fake one, and his limp is such that you might think he's had an injury, but not that his whole foot is missing.

I looked away from his leg back to the sidewalk. A beautiful girl walked by. There had been many. They all looked like they were from Los Angeles or Spain. And the angle from our stairs was very good; you could see a lot of leg and the sides of breasts in loose halter tops. "There certainly are a lot of beautiful girls out here," I said.

"It's what keeps you going," said Chandler. "How often in New York do you have a really gorgeous girl smile at you? It's great. They like the art. They're moved."

I went to get an iced coffee, and when I came back with it, Chandler asked, "You sure you want to drink that? If you're going to drink coffee, I'm going to smoke. I thought I'd quit today, but I say that every day."

For the next two days, Chandler chain-smoked American Spirits, a brand he chooses because the cigarettes are made without chemicals or additives.

"It's my last vice," he said as he enjoyed his cigarette. "I've given up everything. . . . I'm trying to, anyway. Everyone always knew I was a sneaky pervert, but it was okay. I thought it was all right to be a pervert if I was honest about it. But it's not okay. It's my worst vice. If you're going to be a great artist, you have to be a good person. So I'm trying to stop being a pervert."

"What's your perversion?"

"I can be honest with you. I've read your work. I know you won't judge me. I'm a voyeur. But I'm not a sneaky voyeur. I'm an in-your-face-voyeur."

"You like to spy on women?"

"Yes."

"Do they know you're watching?"

"Oh, yeah. I want them to know. For every voyeur there's an exhibitionist, a voyee. A lot of women don't like it when they find out I'm watching them. But then a lot do. Or they come to like it. It can be kind of healthy. It's like a friendship. It becomes concillated."

"Where do you do this?"

"Mostly I go to the roof of my building. I always gravitate toward roofs."

"So they know you're watching? They don't call the police?"

"No. I can't believe it, but I've never been arrested."

"Do they strip for you?"

"Some do. And I like to be naked for them. I walk around naked on my roof or in my apartment. I don't know what the neighbors think. They must be like, There's that lonely, naked, one-legged guy again. For a while I had these Dutch girls as roommates and they walked around naked. It was great. The neighbors probably loved it. It's okay when there are beautiful girls. But now it's just me again, a lonely, naked guy."

"So you're a voyeur *and* an exhibitionist, a combination."

"You could say that."

"When you're naked and looking at the women, do you masturbate?"

"No, that's being a wanker. I don't want to be a wanker. I want to keep it healthy. I don't want to scare them off. I like it to be concillated."

"What's this word, *concillated?* What's it mean? Are you sure it's a word?"

"I don't know, I heard it once. I always think of it. For me it means that they want to do it, too. . . . I recently started something with this new voyee. She's an older woman, in her fifties, but beautiful. She's in the building behind mine. I watch her several nights a week when she comes home from work. She undresses for me. I set up a tent on my roof and I lie in there and watch her and she looks at me. One time she was on the phone and I had my cordless phone with me. And while she talked, I pretended to be talking to someone. I wanted to be doing what she was doing. But who was I talking to? God? It's gotten pretty intense with her. She started touching her breasts the other night and she was looking right at me. I was lying in my tent and I got erect and started fondling myself."

"Wait a second, you told me you didn't wank!"

"It was social wanking. It was concillated."

"That's bullshit," I said. "Wanking is wanking."

Chandler laughed. "You're right, I am a wanker. But I don't want to be. It's bad. I feel sick after I do it. Debauched. I hate myself. But it's because there's been no sales, and when there's no sales, I can't paint, I can't buy materials. I get so frustrated. I figure I might as well go up on the roof. I sleep up there. They see me naked in the morning. . . . I've always thought there was a curious connection between exhibitionism and art. The more frustrated I get with not being able to paint or show my work, the more prolific I become with the exhibitionism. It's a way to have an exhibit. . . . I used to think the sicker you are, the better the art. I wanted to be the best, so I took the sickest road and now I can't get off."

"When you're up there in your tent, are you in a trance?" I asked. "I know when I'm in my sex perversions I call it the sex trance, and nothing can shake me from it."

"Oh, yeah, when I'm doing it, lying there naked watching her, I could die in that moment. I don't need anything else."

Chandler's voyeurism/exhibitionism is not limited to rooftops. Every few months, if he has some extra money, he takes a train out of the city, either two hours to the west or an hour to the north.

He finds small industrial towns and he looks for a hotel, preferably one with a courtyard where he can look into windows. These towns provide him fresh locations for his paintings and for his perversion—hotels have lots of voyeuristic opportunities, and also he likes to be found naked in his bathtub by maids.

"It's a water-purity thing. I'm debauched and cleansed at the same time, neutralized," he said. "And it's also an ethnic prejudice thing with the Spanish maids, which I feel bad about. . . . But at least I'm not perverted around kids. Even my mother said, 'You're not at all creepy around children.'"

"What kind of backwards compliment is that?" I asked. "She's praising you for not being a pedophile. I guess she was trying to look on the bright side."

"I guess she was," Chandler laughed. "She senses that I'm the sneakiest one in the family, and we have a pretty weird family."

In addition to rooftops and hotels, Chandler also likes to exhibit himself while driving. Two years ago, on two hits of Ecstasy and dozens of cups of coffee, he drove to Seattle in three days; he was naked the whole time. "I would stalk cars to find someone, a woman, to look in. I was fondling myself and driving. Sometimes they would look in and smile, sometimes they would look in with disgust. The Ecstasy and the coffee caused the masturbation, I think, and the danger factor that I might be caught and killed was appealing."

"What do you think your face looked like when you pulled alongside those cars?"

"Terrible, frightening," he said.

Like most perverts—like myself—Chandler has periods of great self-loathing and wants to be punished for his actions. For many years he had a fantasy of going to the roof of the Novotel hotel in

Midtown and sitting on the ledge and then just slipping off to the alleyway thirty-three stories below. And he pictured the alleyway instead of the street so that he wouldn't land on anyone.

His exhibitionism is not without consequences. A recent girl-friend broke up with him because she perceived him to be a failure as an artist, and also his so-called friends told her about his visits to the roof. And one time in a hotel in Arkansas, on his way to meet another girlfriend's parents, he was in his bathtub and he looked out his narrow window and he saw a woman walking quickly down the street. He stood up in his bathtub, hoping that she might glance up and see him through the small window, and he fell in the tub. He severely sprained his good ankle and had to meet his girlfriend's parents with a painful double limp.

His exhibitionism began when he was fourteen years old. He would go to this one shoe store where the clerk was a woman. He would wear shorts but no underwear. When the woman would put the shoes on his feet, she would glance up his leg and see his testicles. He went to this store for a number of years. Later, as an adult, he would do the same thing on bus and train rides and hope that girls would look up his shorts.

"That's horrible," I said. "That's the grossest sight in the world. The balls look like red growths. It sickened me when I was on sports teams and we'd be stretching and I'd see everyone's testicles."

"I know it's horrible," Chandler said. "I'm the worst exhibitionist I know. But one time in Oregon on a train this girl liked it and we ended up making out in the bathroom."

"If you're going to get over this," I said, "you can't think of the success stories. What I try to do is think of how low and disgusting I feel afterward. It works about half the time."

"I do that," said Chandler. "The other thing is to come up with healthy expressions of it. I still like to be naked, I think it's beautiful, but I can go to nudist colonies instead of my roof. And if I want to look at a naked woman, I can just hire a model. But I'm so sick—I had this model one time and she was beautiful, lying right in front of me. But I was looking past her out the window across the street to a fogged-over window where I could see just a little bit of a woman's leg, and I kept looking out the window and ignoring the beautiful girl right in front of me."

"How do you think all of this got started?"

"My parents' divorce when I was fourteen, but mostly it's because of my puberty."

"Oh, my God, I forgot. That's right—you didn't start until you were twenty-one. Of course, it makes perfect sense; you want the world to know that you've matured, that you have pubic hair. Did you ever go to a doctor to find out why it was taking you so long?"

"No. My dad kept saying, 'Don't worry, you're going to look young when you're old.'"

"How did you deal with it? I couldn't take showers with other men for years."

"I tried to take a shower once in high school. I was a jock, a top wrestler at one hundred and four pounds, I figured I could do it. But the wimpiest kid in the school came up to me and said, 'Hey, hairy,' because I had no hair. And my balls were up, hidden and small. That still happens to them when I drink coffee."

I was finishing up my iced coffee and I could feel my hemorrhoid worsening, but my balls weren't elevating.

"That must have been humiliating," I said.

"I tried a lot of things to make it look like I had hair after that. I glued on Barbie doll wigs, but they fell off and didn't look very good. And I tried mascara, but sweat would make that run off. One time, I was in our basement and there was this window and I was gluing on a Barbie doll wig and this guy walked by and looked down at me. I felt gross, but it excited me, too."

"That and the shoe store were early important experiences."

"I think so. I remember both very vividly."

"So this is interesting," I said. "Your late puberty sent you into exhibitionism. And my late puberty, according to my counselor, contributed to my fascination with transsexuals. He says that because I was in limbo and unsure of my sexuality and gender during a crucial time, that to this day I identify with transsexuals, who represent this limbo period. But I seem to be outgrowing it now, finally. I simply appreciate transsexuals."

"I think I could get into transsexuals," he said.

I felt a little territorial. "You better stick to one problem," I said. I had been with Chandler for several hours at this point and I needed to go home. I told him I'd return the next day.

"Do you feel okay about all this talking?" I asked.

"I feel great," he said. "It's good to confess to someone."

"I'm glad," I said. "I'm probably going to write this all up. Is that all right?"

"Everyone knows it anyway. It's good to get the truth out. And the I Ching says that to be the clown is the wisest path and that the critics are the real fools."

The second day I was with him, Chandler was wearing shorts. A black elastic knee brace kept his flesh-colored prosthesis attached to his still-healthy thigh. We sat on the concrete stairs. Our legs were splayed out. "I see you're wearing shorts. You better have underwear on," I teased.

"I do. I have boxers on," he said.

"Your testicles can slip out of boxers," I said.

He smiled at me sheepishly. "I'm trying," he said.

Then we started talking quite a lot and I got his life story. Born in Great Falls, Montana, and raised in Tacoma, Washington. Mixed background: Irish, American Indian, Southern Baptist. The youngest of six children. Moved with his mother to Shaker Heights, Ohio, after his parents' divorce. Went to art school in Kansas City and California. Spent his summers working for his father on the Weyerhauser Railroad in the Pacific Northwest, loading ties, pounding spikes. After art school, he lived in L.A. for four years. Spent a year as a small-time flimflam man. That came to an end when he stole a Chinese artifact, a scroll, from the Berkeley Museum. He arranged to sell it on the black market for five thousand dollars but chickened out. A year later, he tried to return it and claim the reward. He said it had been given to him by a girl. He was arrested and in the interrogation room they asked repeatedly, "Harry Chandler, did you steal the scroll?" He broke down after thirty minutes. He spent some time in jail and most of the charges were dropped. The judge ordered him out of the state of California, but he stayed. He made the newspapers: ARTIST STEALS ART.

He got married and ran an awning repair business and destroyed several famous Los Angeles awnings after using an improper sealant. Moved to Rhode Island with his wife. After a year in R.I., they moved to Wilmington, North Carolina, to try to get into the movie business down there. Their marriage was breaking up and his wife was taking care of a dog actor (a dog trained for movies) and the dog pushed her down a flight of stairs and she broke her arm in seven places. Chandler hadn't made it with the studios in Wilmington, so he was leading illegal tours of an old, haunted Masonic temple. He believes that he insulted the ghosts present in the temple, causing disasters for him and his wife. The week after his wife broke her arm, he was at a party at a beach house drinking tequila. After two bottles, Chandler took off all his clothes. He went running out of the house and down a road to the ocean and stepped in a hole and snapped his leg back one hundred and eighty degrees. Drunk, he popped it back in place, but he couldn't walk. He was taken to Cape Fear Hospital.

"This Southern doctor said to me, 'You had enough alcohol to kill a man. You were nekked on the beach. My assistant is going to amputate you at the knee. I'm going fishing.' They called my mother for permission. They said, 'Do you have a son Larry Chandelier?' But she wouldn't let them do it. I was taken in a helicopter to Duke, where maybe they could save the leg, but the gangrene had already set in. I watched my foot turn black over a month."

Over the next two years, Chandler lived in Durham and had fifteen operations on his leg.

"They say you lose five years of your life for every operation. That makes me a hundred and three. I look pretty good for my age, but my immune system was killed by all the morphine. That's why I have so many allergies. And it's why I'm so thin. I don't retain any vitamins, but the herbs are building me back up. But for years I've felt like the man who fell to earth. Getting thinner, dying . . . They cut off my foot on my twenty-ninth birthday. It was powerful astrologically; nines are birth years, can be a good thing—you start over. For me it was a bad thing."

"Did you ever think of suing? There was that hole in the road."

"No, I don't want to sue anyone. . . . I've been receiving disability for ten years, though. Five hundred dollars a month. It's supplemented my art career. I can survive on almost nothing. It's great to be supplemented—I can just paint. It's worked out quite nicely, actually. I could almost say that it's worth it."

After Durham, Chandler came to New York. He lived in an SRO hotel, and before he started selling his paintings on the street, he worked as a bartender. He's had twenty-seven restaurant jobs. One night while bartending on the Upper West Side, he was arm wrestling a patron and his arm was snapped in half. He thought he was going to lose his arm, but he didn't.

At the end of our second day together, Chandler packed up his paintings and table and managed to get it all on a small luggage carrier. He'd had no sales all weekend.

I walked with him while he wheeled his paintings to his loft in Tribeca. On Church Street, a famous painter staggered out of a bar, incredibly drunk, and he hailed Chandler: "There's a real artist!" We shook hands with the drunk and went to Chandler's building. In his vestibule there's a window that faces the street. Chandler hung one of his smaller paintings in the window; underneath the painting, stenciled on the glass, is *Harry Chandler. Paintings. 966-6113.*

We carried his large paintings up to his loft, which he shares with three roommates. In his room, which is also his studio, he showed me many of his paintings and his cutouts—paintinglike depictions made from slices of colored paper.

For several years, Chandler was a regular at the Blue Angel strip club. They let him in for free and he would paint and draw. They hung his work on their walls. He's the Degas of strippers—he has many portraits and nude studies of the girls: It's his Blue Angel period. There are also dozens of his New York street scenes. His paintings are raw and they're full of sex, but there's also an undeniable sadness in his work. His subjects are always remote, lost, lonesome, looked at from a distance.

We went up to his roof to see if his voyee was there, but she wasn't. I saw his yellow pup tent. He told me that I could come up there sometime and lie in his tent and pretend to be him and that she would strip for me. I told him I'd take him up on it.

"So you walk around here nude? I still think it's amazing that no one calls the police."

"The police know about me. They see me from their helicopters. It's okay to be naked in New York City."

He paused a moment, contemplating the legality of what he does, and then he added, matter-of-factly, "But an erection is a felony."

The next day, Chandler came over to my apartment to give me a painting. He also brought over something for me to rub into my scalp to grow hair, and an herb for my hemorrhoid. I thanked him for his presents and he was sitting on my bed and I said, "I'm going to write about you, so I'd like to see your stump."

He rolled up his pants and removed his prosthesis. His stump was covered with layers of socks for padding. He leaned the prosthesis against my bed and it looked like the sawed-off leg of a mannequin. The calf part, he explained, is stiffened fiberglass and it's hollow and Chandler puts his stump inside. The foot part is rubber and very realistic looking. "It's top of the line, made in Seattle," he said. "There's even a thong split for the toes for wearing sandals, and there are toenails and even veins."

He slowly removed the socks from the stump and piled them neatly on my bed; there were at least ten pairs. "I usually have special stump socks, but they get dirty. This stump can really get smelly. Like rotten sauerkraut. Most of the time, I can't smell it, I'm used to it. These kids I teach on Fire Island, I don't know how they put up with it—cigarette breath, rotten stump sauerkraut smell. I guess they must really like me."

He removed the last sock and held his stump in his hand for me to look at. He rubbed the heel to show me how cushiony it was—

the doctors were able to save his heel. His stump looked like a bone with no meat, only skin. The heel was like a rubber stopper at the bottom of a cane.

Chandler was smiling at me. He looked handsome. He lay back on my bed and extended out his stump. "It's not bad," he said. "It's like a fifteen-inch penis. I wish I had *this* back in high school."

Roxanne of the Jersey Shore

I WAS EIGHTEEN, and in the middle of July of 1982, I was down
at Seaside Park, New Jersey, for the weekend. A friend and I had
rented a twenty-dollar-a-day room overlooking the boardwalk, the
beach, and the ocean. We were on top of Mike's Clam on the Half-
Shell, and the smells were perfect for the Jersey Shore: frying grease,
old fish, and ocean breeze.

We lay on the beach sunburning ourselves all day on Saturday,
and then late in the afternoon, we went to our room and drank
beer, which I had managed to buy with my older sister's doctored
driver's license (I had changed her name from Donna to Donald).

Our room had one big double bed and we sat on it and wiped
our sandy feet along the walls. Many others had done this before us
and the walls were covered with footprints.

Around my fourth beer, I was feeling pretty good and I leaned
my head out the window and I saw two girls walking up the boardwalk in that beautiful six-o'clock-in-the-evening sunlight. They
were wearing tank tops and their shoulders were dark brown and
they had trim teenage figures.

"You want to drink some beer?" I called out to them.

I was expecting to get the finger.

"Sure," one of them called out.

"You do? . . . Well, come on up!" I said, and I pointed at the wooden staircase on the side of the clam bar.

"No, you come down."

"All right."

I told my friend what was going on. We both couldn't believe what was happening. It was a Jersey Shore dream. Two girls wanted to drink beer with us. We quickly put on our jeans and washed our faces in the bathroom in the hall. I put the beer in a paper bag and we flew down the wooden steps.

The girls were gone.

We started walking up the boardwalk. We both knew that we weren't cool enough to have a Jersey Shore dream. We sat on a bench. We stared at the ocean. Our young souls had been so happy in those brief moments of putting on our jeans and washing our faces.

We'd been sitting there about five minutes when I happened to glance over my friend's shoulder and I saw the girls approaching us. The cuter of the two was carrying a little brown bag.

"We went to get a bottle of rum from my brother," she said. I was so happy that I probably had a growth spurt. I was only eighteen and didn't reach my full height until I was twenty.

The four of us went and hid under a pier and we drank our beer and rum. Eventually we paired off. I was better-looking than my friend, and I ended up with the very cute girl, who actually had the name of Roxanne. She had honey-blond hair and she was waif-like, with delicate features and a rose of a mouth. She did have a strong Jersey accent, stronger than mine, but I didn't hold that against her.

My friend's girl had an all-right body, but she had bad teeth, which made her face sort of jowly, not pretty. My friend was pissed off that I got Roxanne, but I was lead dog in our little male pack of two, so I got the better girl.

Roxanne and I started making out and grinding into the wet sand. My friend put his arm around his girl and the two of them stared at the surf.

When it was fully dark out, we all went up to the boardwalk and played some of the games in the stalls. We took secret sips from the rum and Roxanne and I were holding hands. I felt on top of the world. I tried to win her a stuffed animal but failed.

When we were all bored with the games, I went to my car and got two blankets and I bought some more beer. We put the two blankets on the beach about twenty feet apart. Roxanne and I made out and my friend and his girl sat on their blanket and didn't kiss. It was a little depressing to feel their gloom so nearby.

I said to Roxanne, "Do you want to go to my room?"

She did. I was having the best Jersey Shore dream possible. We got to the room and I kept the lights off so that she wouldn't see so clearly all the foot marks on the walls. There was a nice silvery light coming in the window from the boardwalk, and the footprints were obscured and looked perhaps like a wallpaper design.

The bed felt wonderful after being on the beach and we held one another and she was a gorgeous young girl. She was only sixteen and her shirt came off and her erect nipples were like extra-long rubber pencil erasers. They stuck out at least an inch and a half from her tiny, nearly flat chest. I hadn't seen many nipples in my life, but I knew that these were unusual. (In fact, I've never seen nipples like that again.)

So it was a little freakish, but also very inspiring. Her pants came off and there were no panties. It was the greatest night of my life. I lavished her whole body and the pencil erasers with kisses. In the nooks and crannies of her knees and elbows and in the sweet pucker of her belly button, I tasted Hawaiian Tropic suntan oil, and it was like an aphrodisiac.

"You can do it," she said.

It. I had only done it with two girls, and that had been after months of dating. And here above the boardwalk in Seaside Park, with the smell of frying clams in the air, a girl I had just met who had the longest nipples in the world was offering herself to me.

I kneeled above her and she opened her thin, smooth legs in a shy and endearing way. I peered down at her in the silvery light. I was nervous—I had made love maybe ten times in my life and had almost always experienced premature ejaculation—but I was also happy.

"Just pull out before . . . you know . . ." she said.

I lowered myself and I kissed her and I was about to enter her when there was a fierce banging on the door, and then I heard my friend say, "I'll go in." And then he was in the room, staring at me. I rose up and was kneeling between Roxanne's legs. Roxanne screamed and covered herself with the pillow.

"Oh, my God," my friend said. He was a virgin.

"GET THE HELL OUT OF HERE," I said. I've never been quick to anger, but this was one moment when I did feel rage, rather than depression, which is my usual response to conflict.

He backed out, a goofy smile on his face, and I felt sort of proud that he was really seeing what a lead dog I was. As soon as he closed the door, Roxanne's girlfriend with the funny jowls started screaming, "What's he doing in there? He's raping her."

Roxanne closed her legs and started crying.

No, I thought, this can't be. "We can still do it," I said to her.

The girlfriend was banging on the door. "Roxanne! Roxanne!"

"I'll be right out," Roxanne screamed through her tears.

"I'm coming in," said the girl, but there was some scuffling outside the door; my friend was obviously keeping the girl away from the door handle. I still had a chance. I was still maintaining my erection. Roxanne scooted to the end of the bed and started pulling on her pants.

"Let's do it really quick," I said. It was going to be quick anyway.

"No," she said angrily.

The halter top came on, the nipples were somehow pressed down, no one would suspect what odd treasures were hidden there.

"Are you all right, Roxanne?" the girlfriend called out.

"I'm all right," she answered.

She began to tie one of her sneakers, she was about to leave me, but I was still naked and still crazy with desire.

"Could you give me a blowjob?" I asked in a sympathetic voice. I thought this was the kind of thing that a man might request under these circumstances. Also, I wanted to be able to report to my friend and to my friends back home that I had scored something significant on a dream of a Jersey Shore night.

"Fuck you," she said, and she stood up and slapped me; it hardly caught my chin and it didn't hurt.

"I'm sorry," I said. "I didn't think it was a bad thing to ask. I didn't mean to be rude. . . . Could I have your address? I'll write you."

She sat back down and she tied her other sneaker. She stood up to leave.

"Please, could I have your address?"

She scrawled it on a piece of paper for me.

"I like you," I said. She didn't say anything back.

She left the room and I wrapped a towel around my waist and sat on the bed. My friend, the idiot, came into the room.

"Why did you come back here?" I asked.

"That girl said she was going to go to the police if I didn't bring her here. We saw a cop on the boardwalk. She thought you were raping her."

We were silent. There were a few beers left. We started drinking them.

"Did you do it?" he asked.

"I was about to when you walked in. I was so close to having sex and you wrecked it."

He was happy. He was glad that I hadn't gotten laid. He didn't like being the number-two dog. And in my own way I was sort of relieved. I knew I would have come in two seconds and disappointed her. I forgave my friend for coitus-interrupting-us.

We put our dirty feet up on the wall and rubbed them up and down. "Did you see her nipples?" I asked.

"No," he said. "I was looking at your ass. You looked really funny. Your ass is really white."

The next day we went home and I wrote Roxanne a long love letter. I apologized for how things had gone awry and for my horrible request of a blowjob, without calling it a blowjob. I wrote: "I'm sorry I asked for what I asked for."

I also proposed in the letter that we get together, that I come visit her.

But she never wrote me back.

So many a night for many years when I needed to come up with something, I would fantasize about completing what she and I had started that one summer night on the Jersey Shore. It was a potent image, and it never took me very long, about as long as it would have lasted then, and I would shudder and see photographs in my mind of those elongated nipples and the shy spreading of her legs.

I Shit My Pants in the South of France

I HAD MY FIRST COLONIC the other day, and for me, it was a dream come true. I've wanted a colonic for the last ten years, but I kept denying myself something that I needed. I do the same thing with shoes—I can't buy a new pair or have the soles replaced until I'm practically barefoot. But you can't treat your colon as shabbily as a pair of shoes, you can't leave it overnight with a cobbler, so I finally broke down and went to a colon hygienist in SoHo. I envisioned my colonic as a sort of fall cleaning—a getting ready for the new 1997 school year, though I'm no longer in school.

I should mention that the week before my appointment, I took a lot of fiber supplements and ate mostly fruits and vegetables. I was trying to purify myself before I went to the hygienist because I didn't want to be embarrassed. I was like a woman cleaning her house before the maid arrives.

But the hygienist turned out to be a nonjudgmental fellow. Bowel cleansing is his business and his name is Ismail. He's a short, kind, radiant man from Uganda. He has a feminine smile, the likes of which I've only seen in photographs of enlightened nuns.

His office is incredibly tiny—it's the size of a walk-in closet. There's room for the bed you lie on, and that's about it. On the walls are articles about the colon and numerous letters from grateful patients. Above the bed are two square plastic containers with water whooshing around inside. They're like the containers, filled with purple- and red-colored drinks, that one sees in old-fashioned diners. But Ismail's containers don't hold artificial grape juice; inside them is the filtered water that is pumped into one's colon via hoses and tubes.

Ismail had me undress and put on a medical gown in the tiny bathroom attached to his office. Then it was onto the bed, where I lay on my side with my back to him. He discreetly parted my gown and inserted a lubricated tube and I wanted to suck my thumb.

He began to pump water inside me and then he reached around me and massaged my intestines in the area just above the groin. When I was really filled up, he hit some kind of switch and the water was let out and released into a big plastic bag at the end of the bed. Essentially, I was defecating in Ismail's compassionate presence.

"I'm going to find all your treasures," he said, and then he asked, "What do you do for a living?"

"I'm a writer."

"I'd like to write a book," he said. "The things I've seen. I have one woman who I call the Animal Kingdom Lady."

"Why?"

"She came in here and I asked her, 'How often do you go?' She said, 'Every two months.' I didn't think I heard her right, so I said, 'Every two days?' She said, 'No.' I said, 'Every two weeks?' She said, 'No, every two months.' Can you believe it?"

"Wow, she must have been really impacted. But why do you call her the Animal Kingdom Lady?"

"I was pumping her out, and after twenty minutes, I told her to go sit on the toilet and rest. She was in there and then I heard screams. I opened the door, and she was shouting, 'Bugs! Bugs!'

In the toilet were five or six giant parasites swimming. I flushed them down!"

"How big were they?" I asked, horrified.

He spread his fingers and indicated a size of at least six inches. "My God," I said. "How did she survive with those things inside her? I guess they left her a few crumbs to live on and took the rest of the food for themselves. That's why she hardly ever went to the bathroom. They were eating all her food. Freeloaders! The bastards!"

Ismail was impressed with my deductive reasoning. It seems I'm a natural when it comes to the intestines. And adventurous too. I'm sort of the George Plimpton of the colon—one of my motivations for going to Ismail was so that I could write about the experience. It's scatological *participatory journalism,* but each writer must find his or her domain.

In speaking with Ismail about the bug lady, I further showed my flair for the subject by guessing that the parasites looked like spiders, which was correct. And Ismail, impressed again by my savvy, explained to me that New Yorkers are loaded with parasites and worms that they get from bad meat and fish. And suddenly the whole city felt like a place infested with bugs, inside and outside of us—just that morning I had lifted up my hat from the kitchen table and two cockroaches, probably teenagers necking, had scampered away.

Ismail sensed my darkening mood and he said, hoping to distract me, "You're a writer, tell me a story."

So I told him the following tale, which I thought he would appreciate: In 1983, I spent the summer with a good friend in the South of France taking classes. I was good-looking then, with a full head of blond hair, and one night my friend and I were in a café with three lovely Dutch girls. They were praising me endlessly, telling me that I looked like a young Robert Redford and that someday I would be famous. I was loving it, and my friend had to tolerate me getting all the attention. Then the evening wound down and the five of us only had enough money for the girls to take a cab back to the dormitory, where we were all staying.

Off they went and my friend and I started walking home. A dirty man standing in front of a café offered me a tuna sandwich that was resting in the palm of his hand—*sans* napkin. I had a few centimes left and I was hungry and I bought the sandwich. My judgment was impaired—I was drunk from the praise of the girls and the beer we had been drinking. I ate the sandwich. My friend and I continued walking, and five minutes later I was convulsed in pain and had the most overwhelming need to shit that I had ever experienced in my life. We started to run back to the café.

"I'm not going to make it!" I shouted. "That sandwich!"

"Maybe if we stop running," my friend said.

I stopped and immediately exploded with diarrhea like a ruptured sewer main. "I shat in my pants!" I wailed. I had never used the past tense before. My friend crumpled to the ground laughing.

I limped into an alleyway, removed my pants, took off my underwear, which was filled like a baby's diaper, and I hid the revolting package under a parked Peugeot. I pulled my pants back up and my legs and ass were vilified and slick.

We went back to the taxi stand. I was walking very slowly. We planned to take a cab to the dorm and then my friend would run to our room and get money for the driver. We got in a taxi, I thought everything was going to be all right, and then my own smell came to my nose and my friend's nose. We quickly rolled down the windows, but then the stink made it to the front seat. The taxi driver whipped his head around and looked right at me, following the odor's vaporous trail. In French, he shouted at me, "You shit in my car like a dog."

He made an immediate U-turn back to the taxi stand and told all the other drivers I had shit in my pants and not to take me in their cars. Humiliated, my friend and I walked home. It was a two-mile journey and my legs were encrusted. Just as I approached the dorm, salvation, I convulsed and shit again in my pants. Robert Redford, my ass!

I finished my story and Ismail, weak from laughter, was leaning his head tenderly on my hip. We felt very close to each other. At the end of the session, we hugged good-bye.

I walked through SoHo and I experienced the most profound happiness. I was relieved of all tension and anxiety—it was magnificent. My colon was clean, my spirit was light.

I then headed up Fifth Avenue for an appointment at a publishing house. I was going to see a friend of mine, an editor, because her publisher wanted to meet me. He wasn't going to publish my new book, due to come out next August, but he was a fan of my work in the *Press* and had heard that I'd sold a novel. My friend brought me to the publisher's beautiful corner office and the man offered me a gourmet cheese stick.

"No, thank you," I said. I didn't want a cheese stick right after my colon had been cleaned, but the man, a good person, insisted. How could I refuse? How could I tell a stranger I'd just had a colonic?

So I munched on the cheese stick while the publisher praised my work, and then suddenly I felt a crushing spasm in my colon. I was still pumping out water that Ismail had injected me with. I was overwhelmed with the need for release. Sweat jettisoned out of my bald spot. The publisher told me again that he loved my work. I didn't think my sphincter would hold. I was going to crap in my pants in a publishing house as I was being praised. Couldn't I have one moment in the sun? I felt faint. It was Robert Redford all over again. Then the publisher had to take a phone call and I whispered to my friend that I needed a toilet. I rushed down the hall and made it just in time.

A half hour later, I was walking home on Fifth Avenue. The spasms hit me again. Hard. I fought them and I lost. I shat. People in their fancy clothes walked past me unawares. I craned my neck and on the seat of my pants was a big wet spot looking like a Rorschach blot. I deciphered it's simple psychological message: You're a loser.

This Other Side of Paradise

M Y FIRST REAL LOVE was a girl named Claudia. She was a big blonde with big green eyes. We met the first week of our freshman year at Princeton. She was only seventeen, and during those first days of school at the end of summer, she was terribly homesick for Southern California, where she had grown up on the beach with her surfing brothers, wild sisters, and hard-drinking father. Her mother had fled the father when Claudia was young, leaving behind five kids.

We met at a dance the second night of Freshman Week. She was beautiful, but also very sad, and I wanted to take care of her right away. She was longing desperately for the ocean, had never been apart from it her whole life, so we skipped orientation the next day and I bought us bus tickets for Atlantic City. It was the only beach in New Jersey that you could get to from Princeton using public transportation. So we sat on that bus early in the morning and she leaned her head against my shoulder and she slept. I'd never had a girl lean against me like that, like I was someone who could be counted on. We hadn't kissed the night before because she had mentioned a boyfriend back in California. So I had nobly thought that I would just have to be a friend to this beautiful girl, and as she slept, it felt like the most important thing in the world not to move, not to disturb her. And I remember it was kind of uncomfortable to be so still, but that it was a beautiful discomfort because I was a martyr and already in love.

When we got to Atlantic City, the driver gave us a ten-dollar roll of quarters for gambling—everyone on the bus got such a roll— and we went right from the bus into a casino. We didn't even see the ocean. I played one hand of blackjack and doubled our money. I quit right then and felt like a big shot. We went outside and walked down the glorious wide boardwalk. Claudia had never seen the Atlantic before. It was an overcast day, and the Atlantic was gray and heavy-looking, but she thought it was beautiful. And I felt like an even bigger shot—I had given her the ocean.

We bought sandwiches and fruit with our gambling money and had a picnic on the beach. We had both worn our bathing suits under our clothes and she was in a skimpy bikini. She was only seventeen, but she was full-hipped and large-breasted and gorgeous. She lay on her towel, her face to the meager sun, and I lay on my belly with a hard-on drilling into the sand. We dipped in the water once or twice, but it was cold.

Around four o'clock we left the beach and we found this old lady's house where you could shower and change for five dollars. There was a sign on the porch: $5 SHOWERS. It was 1982 and I guess Atlantic City still had old ladies then who rented out their bathrooms. She asked us if we were married—if you were married, you could both be in the little changing room (a bedroom) at the same time—and Claudia said yes, surprising me. We got in the room and she stripped right in front of me, and I turned away like a gentleman, but I caught a glimpse of pink nipples, a honey-colored mound. I thought she must not be shy because she was from California. She went into the shower and then she called to me, why don't I join her. I had never showered with someone before, and I went in shyly, nervously. We had our first kiss.

That night back at Princeton we made love, and she told me that it was over with her boyfriend back in California. We quickly became famous in our dormitory for screwing all the time. I was eighteen and I think it was the best sex of my life because I trusted her and I hadn't yet twisted up my soul. When we'd make love, I'd go into some dark, black fantastical place, like a falling or a flying, and there was this deeply pleasing loss of self-consciousness.

As winter came, her homesickness returned and she was mournfully sad. Her hair started turning brown. She hated the cold. At times she'd become so quiet, almost mute. She was the middle child in her big alcoholic family—her older brothers got drunk with the father every night—and she was an expert at disappearing. But she also missed her crazy family, needed them.

Christmas break came and I called her every day in California. Then she wasn't there for a week, but she hadn't told me she was going anywhere. I spoke to one of her sisters and she said that Claudia was in Mexico. That was a miserable week for me and we didn't speak again until I saw her our first night back in Princeton. She confessed that she had gone to Mexico with her old boyfriend, but now it was over for good. Then she told me everything. Turned out her old boyfriend was a thirty-five-year-old man, a teacher at her high school. She had been sleeping with him since she was fifteen. She had hid all this from me. I hated this unknown man for being a law-breaking bastard, and I also felt betrayed by Claudia. We didn't break up or anything, but something strange happened during our sex. I couldn't lose myself anymore. I felt this barrier between our bodies even if I was pressed right against her, and sixteen years later I've never again been able to lose myself with a woman the way I did with her in the beginning.

Then during the spring of that year, Claudia learned some-thing—if she flirted with other guys, I went into a rage. At this one party, she let some jerk grab her right in front of me and I threw him onto a pool table and I put my forearm to his throat. I had to be pulled off him. I was a strong kid then.

We tried to fix things up. Claudia had a camera and this one morning we took these nude pictures of each other. Then we bor-rowed a car and we went back to the Jersey Shore and we took pic-tures on the beach. And the little trip to the ocean made things better for a few weeks, but then this one night we didn't go out together and we went to different parties and I cheated on her and she cheated on me. In the morning, after being with this other girl, I realized how much I loved Claudia and I went to tell her that I loved her, but she was all sick and hungover, and before I could say anything, she told me that she had slept with someone. Then she told me that she had lost the camera with our pictures inside it. She thought she'd left the camera with the guy. I got his name out of her and I called him and asked him if he had her camera. My plan was to get the camera and to beat him up. He said he didn't have it. And it didn't seem like I could just go to his room and attack him. So I almost busted my hand punching Claudia's wall. The camera was never found. And I didn't confess *my* betrayal.

We stayed together a few more weeks, and then summer came. We didn't see each other for all of June or July, but then at the beginning of August we both had managed to get to Europe and we met up in Vichy, France. When she was out of the room where we were staying, I read her diary. She had cheated on me again. I broke up with her. I learned to never read another person's diary.

Sophomore year, she started sleeping with a friend of mine to torture me, and it worked pretty well. Then I took a year off from Princeton in 1984 and I went back to Europe and she followed me.

Now it was my time to torture her. She came all the way to Paris to ask me to take her back, but I wouldn't. For the next couple of years, she always wanted to get back together, but I'd always refuse.

Then in 1987, our senior year, something amazing happened. They were renovating the student center and this girl, who knew Claudia and who was part of the clean-up crew, found in the back of an old cubbyhole an envelope of photos. They were from the lost camera of four years before. Someone had developed the pictures of the two of us naked and then hidden them in that cubbyhole, where they had remained all those years.

Claudia got them from the girl and brought them to me, and the pictures did something to us. We made love for the first time since 1983—and the condom broke. Three weeks later, she was pregnant. We went for counseling and I told her I'd marry her, but I didn't really mean it. She decided to get an abortion. Princeton sent us to a clinic in New York State. It must not have been legal in New Jersey.

We sat in this waiting room in the clinic with teenaged girls and their mothers, and when they called Claudia's name, I said, "I love you."

While she was in there, I went for a walk outside and I was all nervous and distraught and somehow I slipped on some grass. It was muddy and my pants had this long brown streak down the side of my leg and I was mortified. It looked like I had shit, and then when the mud quickly dried, it looked like blood. I couldn't go back inside the clinic. I waited at the glass doors and then I saw Claudia. I went to get her and she was all high on Valium, and to the girls in the waiting room, in this loud, drunk voice, she shouted, "DON'T BE SCARED. YOU DON'T FEEL ANYTHING." I pulled her outside, and then she told me with this goofy smile on her face that the doctor had given her the age of the fetus, and that the dead baby was too old to have been mine.

But then when the Valium wore off, she wouldn't tell me again what the doctor had said. And whenever I brought it up, she'd refuse to talk about it. So I stopped asking her, and I'll simply never know if I made a baby with her. It's easier to think that I didn't.

And she's married now. Has two beautiful children. I met them once. And she and I exchange E-mails every few months.

Girls in My Tub

IN MY SMALL EAST VILLAGE APARTMENT, the bathtub is in the kitchen. I can't shower in my tub, but attached to the faucet is a hose with a showerhead, and I use this to rinse off while I sit there. While bathing, I often think of Henry Roth's beautiful Lower East Side novel, *Call It Sleep*. There's a description of the protagonist's sexy, Oedipal mother washing herself in a tub such as mine, in a kitchen such as mine, at the turn of the century. I scrub my hairy chest and I think of her sponging her beautiful breasts.

Last Sunday morning, I was in the tub and I was working on my head with my scalp invigorator. The rubber hose was lying coiled at the bottom of the tub like a snake; water was jetting out of the showerhead, warming my ankles. Then I nudged the snake and at that precise moment something happened to the building's cold-water supply—it was cut off—and the nudging moved the showerhead so that it was aimed not at my ankles, but at my testicles. My tiny balls were then scalded and I screamed and threw the scalp invigorator into the air.

I quickly shut off the water and stared down at myself. Was I going to have to call 911 for singed testicles? I had heard many stories over the years of children burned in their bathtubs, and then I thought of Henry James and the myth that his testicles had been burned, or punctured on a fence, and this had caused his legendary asexuality—was this to be my fate? But I inspected myself and I didn't seem to be seriously injured, though I was definitely red.

The whole thing was ridiculous—to have one's testicles burned while massaging one's head with a rubber scalp invigorator was a private moment of profound humiliation. I often find such defeats to be more painful than the ones that occur in public—they seem to really tell me who I am, much more than an embarrassing moment in front of others, like slipping on wet stairs.

After this difficult bath, the day unfolded in a slightly insane fashion. I went strolling for a little exercise and I came across my favorite homeless girl. She has sea-green eyes and she's wonderfully beautiful. She's fair and blond and in the summer she would wear a filthy, low-cut gray T-shirt and a black push-up bra. She'd sit under the scaffolding by Cooper Union, waiting for alms, and I would look down at her beautiful dirt-smudged breasts and empty my pockets of all my change. Over time, I spoke to her. She's nineteen, from California, was kicked out of her house at sixteen, and lives with her boyfriend and her dog in the park by the East River. At one time it looked like she and her boyfriend were going to Philadelphia to live with his parents, but that fell through in September.

So I gave her a dollar last Sunday; she was in her usual spot. She was wearing a bulky blue winter coat—there was an early November chill—and I said, to make small talk, "Any chance you'll get to Philadelphia after all? It's getting cold."

"No, his parents don't want us."

"What are you going to do?"

"We're trying to get jobs, but we don't know how to pay taxes. I don't want to be arrested by the government."

"You don't have to worry about taxes," I said, and I looked down at her blond hair; she always parts it in the middle like a Swiss maiden. Her scalp was dirty and red—irritated, probably from lice. As always, I wanted to invite her to come take a bath in my kitchen. She's so dirty, but so beautiful, and after the bath I'd buy her new clothes. And I always think how I'll reassure her that I won't touch her while she bathes, but maybe I'd ask if I could watch. Then I imagine myself at my kitchen table, looking, and she's in the tub glowing, emerging rose-colored—divine. Maybe she would let me take the washcloth, and I reach out to touch . . .

But there my reverie always ends. I worry that I'll be arrested, that she'd come to my apartment and accuse me of rape. So I said good-bye to her last Sunday and left her with her strange, naive worries about taxes.

I went back to my apartment and spent the day reading. Then that night I was feeling restless and empty and odd, and whenever I'm this way, I like to go to Edelweiss, my transsexual bar. I find it calming to be around the girls. I love to watch them, be around them. It's like theater. The bar is on Thirty-ninth Street now; the old grand Edelweiss on Eleventh Avenue was closed down because of prostitution, so it switched locations, trying to stay one step ahead of the police.

My friend Lulu was there, looking sexy and sleek in a black cocktail dress that was only a shade darker than her skin. The bar was smoky and I bought Lulu a drink, and we observed the girls around us. There was a pretty good crowd for a Sunday night, about thirty queens and an equal number of men. My eye was drawn to a stunning blond girl dancing by herself near the stage at the end of the room; she looked eerily like my homeless girl. She was wearing a short white dress and there was absolutely nothing about her that indicated the presence of the Y chromosome. Her breasts jiggled naturally, her legs were lean, her rear shapely, her arms thin. Her face was composed of delicate, attractive features.

"Is that a real girl?" I asked Lulu.

"No, but she's had the surgery," she said. "She had a rich Mafia boyfriend who paid for everything."

We watched her dance and she was spinning around slowly, lost in her own world. "Looks like she's on drugs," I said.

"She's on a lot of stuff," said Lulu. "She's crazy. If you go up to her, she'll show you her pussy. I've seen her do it to a number of guys."

I went and sat at a table near where she was dancing. She didn't look exactly like the homeless girl, but they could have been sisters. I wondered if I could ask *her* to come home with me and watch *her* take a bath. She noticed how I was staring and she sat down with me.

"Buy me a drink," she said. Her eyes were all glazed and drugged. She wanted a rum and Coke. I came back from the bar with her drink. She took several large sips. I gazed at her beautiful face, her full lips. She said, "You know, my brother started raping me when I was nine."

She said this aggressively, trying to shock me, perhaps for staring at her rudely. I didn't say anything—I *was* shocked—and then in a softer tone, as if we had been in the middle of a conversation, she continued, "He did it for years. Every night he came into my room. Then he stopped."

"Why did he stop?" I asked.

"He got a girlfriend, and then he married her."

"How old were you when he stopped?"

"Sixteen."

"Did you try to fight him when he first started?"

"Yeah, but he was big."

"When did you start liking it?" I asked, playing the psychologist, but also thinking how I might have reacted.

She looked at me; her eyes seemed to focus a little. We had been playing a game where she was telling me all these shocking truths, but then *I* said something real. She answered me, "When I was twelve. I'd lie there and wait for him."

"You must have been sad when he got married."

"I didn't go to the wedding. I didn't want to see that bitch. Now I'm prettier than her. Much prettier. I don't know why he stays with her. But he won't even talk to me on the phone. Won't see me. No one in my family will. He should fucking divorce her and marry me."

"You *are* very pretty," I said, as some meager consolation, and I thought sadly how she had turned herself into a woman to win back her brother.

She finished her rum and Coke, and then she said with pride, "I have a pussy. I'm not like the other girls in here." She made a motion with her hand, dismissing the whole bar.

I didn't want to tell her I had been tipped off that she was different, so I just nodded. Then she stood up and lifted her dress, just as Lulu said she would. She had no panties on and she said, "Look." It was dark in the bar, but I could make it out a little. There was the neat triangle of hair, and then there was an opening, an empty space, like in a child's mouth along the gums when a tooth has fallen out. Then she lowered her dress and laughed. She went across the room and started dancing in front of the mirrored wall. She stared at herself.

I stood up and walked to the bar. I said good-bye to Lulu and she asked, "Did she show it to you?" I said yes and I left Edelweiss and went home. I took my second bath of the day. I smelled of cigarette smoke and wanted to get it off me. I was very careful not to burn myself.

Beautiful Again

WHEN I WAS TWENTY YEARS OLD I was beautiful. I didn't know it then, but I was. I have these incredible pictures from that time and I look at them. I was perfect. The pictures are perfect—my youth presented to me like an intact fossil.

How did I come to have these pictures? I was a freshman at Princeton and my best friend kept telling me I should model. I guess he sort of admired me and loved me, in the way that boys sometimes love one another when they are in school together. To him I was heroic-looking. I was very blond and muscular, and he was dark and thin.

So he was always after me to model, and then in the fall of our sophomore year, he did something about it. A photographer was taking pictures of some models, using the Princeton campus as a handsome backdrop, and my friend brazenly approached this photographer and told the man about me and gave him my phone number.

The next day, the man called me. We met for coffee. Right away he told me I could be a model, that I could make lots of money doing it. But he was a strange little fellow. Mid-forties, about five-foot-five, an ugly dark wig on his head, large brown eyes, and a neat mustache. He looked mildly depraved, but he also had charm. Like many photographers, he stared at you in a way that made you feel attractive, gorgeous even. So he appealed to my vanity. "You must have lots of girlfriends," he said. He also said he'd take my pictures for two hundred dollars, and with these photos I could go to a modeling agency in New York and present myself.

I took him up on it, even though in my gut I believed myself to be ugly. I'd always had a very big nose that my face didn't really catch up to until my senior year in high school, and even then I thought it was much too big. So for years I had tried very hard never to be seen from the side—if someone tapped me on the shoulder, I would whip around completely, only showing my profile for an instant. A head-on view, I thought, hid the startling dimensions of my nose, a nose that I was always studying at home in the bathroom mirror, while also using a hand-held mirror so that I could fully diagnose my proboscis from all angles. I would try to convince myself that maybe my nose wasn't so big and ugly, but I never could. Some people suffer from body-image distortion. I had nose-image distortion.

And my father didn't help with my insecurities. When I was growing up, he had three nicknames for me: Oedipus, Dick Tracy, and Ugly. "Hey, ugly, how are you doing?" was the way he would usually greet me when he came home from work. And when I would express my concern about my nose and being ugly, he'd tease me and tell me not to worry because I looked like someone famous—bent-nosed Dick Tracy. My father's logic was inverted. He thought that by calling me Dick Tracy and ugly, he was letting me know that he thought I was beautiful, but when I was a child, I didn't understand his hidden meanings.

So when I was nineteen, hoping to prove that I was perhaps good-looking and not ugly, I went with this odd, wigged photographer to Asbury Park, New Jersey, and had my picture taken. I didn't smile once because I thought smiling made my nose expand, and the photographer took lots of pictures of me, mostly beefcake shots of me shirtless in a pair of jeans, sitting on a jetty.

But after this little adventure in Asbury Park, he disappeared with my two hundred dollars and the undeveloped film. I left phone messages for a few months but eventually gave up. My vanity—actually, profound insecurity—had been taken advantage of. But then in the late spring of that sophomore year, 1984, the pictures arrived in the mail with no explanation as to their delay. I never saw that strange photographer again, but he was a good lensman. I thought for sure that there would be proof of my ugliness inside that envelope he sent me, but when I opened it, to find out what my two hundred dollars had wrought, I was shocked to see how handsome I appeared. Why didn't my nose seem bigger?

So my best friend, who had started this whole mad scheme, urged me to take the pictures to modeling agencies in New York. With school ending for the year, I followed my friend's instructions and looked in the New York yellow pages under "Modeling." And, remarkably, the first little agency I went to out of the phone book took me on, and things happened quickly. A famous photographer, Bruce Weber, chose me for a series that he was doing on athletes, and I qualified as an athlete—I was one of the captains of the Princeton fencing team. So one morning I left New York in a van with several other male models; we were headed for Bruce Weber's home in the country. One of the men, an ex–football player and ex–construction worker, looked at us all in the van and said, noticing for the first time, "Hey, we're all blond!" It wasn't an astute observation, but it was accurate.

Our day in the country, to my English major's eyes, was like something out of Christopher Isherwood's *Berlin Stories.* Amidst these thick pine trees, in this secluded wood, we blond boys were in and out of the pool, swimming, pumping up our muscles, and waiting to have our pictures taken in the late-afternoon light. Bruce, our host, was shy and sweet and gracious. I remember him quietly asking me who my favorite writers were, and I was so nervous in his famous presence that I could hardly speak. I think I said Fitzgerald, which is such a boring and overused answer, no matter how great *The Great Gatsby* is.

He took my picture while I sat in a beautiful wooden swing with a towel around my waist. My bathing suit, hidden by the towel, was pulled down, revealing the flank of my ass, giving the illusion that I was naked. There were several assistants around and Bruce rapidly took many pictures and I noticed that his thumb was oddly misshapen from years of advancing film so furiously.

Then Bruce asked me if I would remove my bathing suit. He was gentle in his request and assured me that I didn't have to. I thought about it for a second and then said I couldn't do it. He didn't ask me why, he was understanding. And my refusal wasn't because of prurience or worry that somehow I would jeopardize my fledgling "career," it was simply because I was concerned that my penis would look small. My neuroses had a certain equilibrium—my nose was too big, my penis too small.

Bruce Weber, though, did cure me of my nose condition. He said that he loved my nose. And the effect was almost immediate— if one of the world's most famous photographers loves your nose, it can't be that bad. Which makes me realize now that I should have taken off my bathing suit—I could have been cured of my penis condition.

So my whole modeling career, which began more or less with this Bruce Weber shoot, lasted all of six weeks. During this time, I was photographed by another fashion legend, a man named Horst, and he took my picture for a Fernando Sanchez lingerie ad. When I was presented to Horst, who must have been in his late seventies, his assistant told me to take off my shirt. I did and I stood before this legendary *Vogue* picture-taker, and the assistant said, "Look, he's like a statue. . . . *And* he speaks French!" Horst didn't say anything, merely smiled. And I was too young to feel humiliated.

For the picture, I was positioned, while wearing only silk red boxer shorts, beneath three very beautiful lingerie-clad women, and the ad appeared several months later in bus stops all over New York City.

I made some nice money from that ad and had one other paid job: modeling a football uniform for a sports-equipment magazine. Ironically enough, the photo shoot was at the Princeton football stadium. I masqueraded as a quarterback at my very own school and got to pretend that I was a Fitzgerald-like hero defeating Yale.

During these six weeks of modeling, whenever I was about to be shown my pictures, like with that first batch of photos, I always thought the jig would finally be up and my inherent ugliness revealed. But each time, these professional wizards with their cameras did something to me, got me at just the right angle, and yet I still didn't believe that I was good-looking. I thought somehow I was pulling some kind of con, maybe because I never smiled. And you can see in my eyes in the pictures a certain fear—a fear that this would be the shot that exposed me for what I was.

So I took the money I made from the lingerie ad and the football ad and went to Europe, taking a year off from Princeton. I was supposed to go to Milan, Italy, and model, but I never showed up. I told myself that it wasn't fitting for someone who wanted to be a writer to model, but really it was because I was scared. I had started drinking a lot and thought I wouldn't be able to fool the camera anymore, since I was so hungover all the time. Also, I had developed a new neurosis—I was convinced that I was starting to lose my hair. My nose-image distortion had simply moved north. I wasn't prematurely balding, I was prematurely *worried* about balding. So I didn't go to Milan. I traveled for three months and then lived in Paris for a while.

I came back to New York in February of '85, and my picture was in Fernando Sanchez bus stop ads all over the city. I stood next to the poster one time, waiting for a bus in a fiberglass shelter on the Upper East Side, and nobody knew that I was the boy lying there in the picture beneath the three beautiful women. And I went to the Whitney Museum Biennial because Bruce Weber was part of the show, he had a whole wall, and there was the picture of me in that swing, my white ass showing. And I saw the other men from that day. Some of them hadn't been afraid that their penises were small.

I was twenty years old and I was lauded for my appearance on the streets and in the museums of New York, but I never tried to model again. And over the next eleven years, my drinking got worse and I sort of ravaged my looks. And I was so nervous all the time about going bald that I probably brought about my worst fear myself—I did get a big bald spot.

So I didn't look at my modeling pictures very often—they made me too aware of how I was squandering my life, my health—but once in a while if I did manage to get a girlfriend, I would often show her the pictures. I was always hoping they would think, Well, he was good-looking once. I guess I'll stick with him. Unfortunately, one of my girlfriends, upon seeing all my old muscles and hair, said, half-jokingly, half-forlornly, "God, you *were* a stud. I wish I could cut your hair out of those pictures and paste it on your bald spot."

I didn't think she was being cruel because I felt the same way. But these days I'm doing better. The drinking problem is for the moment in remission and the hair problem, like the nose problem before it, has started to fade. I don't seem to mind my thin hair.

Currently, I'm not distorting anything too much. But when I look at the modeling pictures, I do feel sad. I pity that pretty boy. He didn't know how lovely he was and I want to save him from what's going to happen. I sort of love him. I remember him. I want him to come back. I must want to be him again. I must want to be beautiful again. What would it be like to be beautiful and know it?

Insomni-Whack

FIRST THERE WAS a homosexual fantasy. It happens whenever I'm low on money. I feel weak, humiliated, pathetic, so then I see an erect organ, not my own, presenting itself. What follows is an imagined moment of cruel sensuality. Then the thought: It would probably hurt. And then I think about disease. By now the whole fantasy is shot, so I'm just sort of beat around the head by the thing or it stares at me in a menacing way. Then I'm reaching for the hand towel, which I've hidden under my pillow, and clean up the unfortunate mess.

It's the same fantasy every time with very little change; it all occurs in a shadowy void, though once in a while there's a prison cell as a backdrop. Last night it happened, and, as always, I regretted the whole thing. But I am weak, weak. Always giving in. I've been destroying my body and my mind and my hair and my soul with masturbation for eighteen years. I'm wasting away. People often say to me: You're so thin. It's because I'm on a steady diet of jerking off. I wonder if it would work for women. I could become rich. Solve my money problems. Write a book encouraging women to lose weight through masturbation.

I tried to fight the urge last night, but I did it because I thought it would help me sleep. And I need sleep. Four nights in a row, I've had terrible, relentless insomnia. It is a symptom of my growing depression, which, like the homosexual fantasies, has been brought on by my financial troubles. Somehow I was doing all right in '97, probably because I received my advance for my second novel, but I've gone through the whole thing, and it wasn't much, and now everything's fallen apart here in early '98. I've paid my January rent, but that's it. Haven't paid the phone bill, electric bill, health insurance, minimum charges on maxed-out credit cards with interest rates at 21 percent, and now I'm getting letters and phone calls about making payments on my enormous graduate school loans. And I don't even remember going to graduate school. It was a three-year drunken blur in the early nineties resulting in a useless degree. It couldn't possibly be worth fifty thousand dollars.

The whole thing is crushing, debilitating. And like all of my problems, it's entirely my fault. So I'm depressed, defeated, morbid, *and* I have insomnia. Each night I've woken up at four A.M. The first night I felt like my whole life was a lie—the kind of thought one has at that hour; the second night I kept saying to myself, Maybe I should just die; and the third night I was resigned and less full of self-pity and I read a whole *New York Press* and the first two chapters of *The Brothers Karamazov.*

Then last night, even after the masturbation, I slept for only a few hours and again woke up at four A.M. I pretended that I must be thirsty and I took a drink from the water bottle next to my bed. Then I closed my eyes. Snuggled against the pillow. But I couldn't fool the insomnia demons. They knew I wasn't parched. Oh, God, I'm up again, I thought. To try to fall back to sleep, I played two of my usual hero fantasies through my head: (1) I save a woman from rape, but I am stabbed by the assailant, though I still manage to knock him unconscious. The police and EMS arrive and I'm rushed to a hospital. I survive, and the next day I'm hailed as a hero on the front pages of the tabloids: WRITER SAVES WOMAN. (2) I wake up one day with incredible jumping powers and I get a tryout with the Knicks, make the team, and I'm hailed on the *back* pages: 5'11" 33-YEAR-OLD WRITER CAN DUNK!

But I was too depressed to really work up the hero stories and fill them with pleasurable details, so I turned on the light and saw the Dostoyevsky, but couldn't face it, the long names. So I read two Graham Greene short stories. The names are easier. And then I was too tired to read anymore, but it wasn't the kind of tired that lets you sleep. That kind of tired is like a book closing gently; insomnia tired is like the pages of the book are slowly burning, curling inward, turning black. There's no rest, just the torture of nerves coming undone, fraying.

So then I started to whack off again. I was hoping that two sessions in a four-hour span would put me out. This time the fantasy was heterosexual. I thought of this unnamed beauty whom I often see on Second Avenue. I imagined us talking on the street. I say to her, "I've seen you for months. I find you very beautiful." She invites me up to her apartment. She lies on her bed. She's naked. My head is between her legs, she pulls me in tight, my nose is inside her. I cry and weep and take comfort in her delicious womb. Then the thought intrudes: Since I've picked her up on the street, she probably hasn't had a chance to shower for a few hours and maybe she'll have a bad urine smell. I don't judge her for this, but what if it's genuinely unpleasant? I push this thought out of my mind, but I seem to take heed in my fantasy. I rise up from her pussy and her arms are over her head. The full bounty of her breasts is revealed to me. I pounce. We join. Splendor. Enchantment. Rapture. I reach for the towel.

The whole thing, like the homoerotic masturbating session, lasted about forty-five seconds. I never give myself any foreplay. I've been prematurely ejaculating while masturbating for years. The images come lightning fast, and then I come lightning fast. As soon as it's over, I don't remember if there was any pleasure. It happens too quick. Also the thing must be worn out like an old needle on a record player. There's probably not much sensitivity left. Masturbation, for me, has become purely a nervous habit, like cracking my knuckles.

I was hoping at least that it would help me sleep—two debilitating releases in four hours—but no, I was wide awake and yet exhausted. I got dressed and decided that I would go to the Kiev and pollute myself with an enormous sleep-inducing meal.

It was five A.M. I trudged up deserted, freezing Second Avenue. I felt limp-dicked from the masturbating. My nostrils burned from the cold. My beautiful woman was asleep somewhere. The avenue was sort of lovely in its emptiness. I bought a *Post*.

Paula Jones was on the cover, and I was saddened. I love Clinton. I once dreamt that he said to me, "You're going to be all right," and it was very reassuring. And I don't care if he's libidinous. Alpha males—leaders—are supposed to be that way. I'm a *zeta male* and *I'm* sex-crazed, so I can imagine that the sex drive at the top of the alphabet must be unbearable.

I went into the Kiev and an adorable, light-haired Polish waitress approached with a menu. "Good morning," she said. "How are you?" Her smile was real, endearing.

"Lousy," I said. "Insomnia." But she was already walking away from me, not listening. I wanted her to mother me. I want all beautiful waitresses to mother me. And they are like mothers—the good ones; they're sweet to you and they bring you food. Just two nights ago, I borrowed some money from a friend and went into a Thai restaurant and ordered a bowl of soup. These two Thai waitresses, with beautiful exposed arms, were so solicitous. I didn't deserve such kindness, I felt. If I could have a harem, I'd compose it with all the beautiful waitresses I've known and worshiped.

I studied the Kiev menu. I decided to get the Breakfast Sampler. It was weighty and noxious: ten slices of kielbasa, bacon, krakus ham, a single pancake, and a piece of French toast. I was raised kosher and I hardly ever eat pork except when I'm feeling self-destructive.

The waitress-angel floated back over. "How's the Sampler?" I asked.

"It's good," she said in her delightful singsong Polish accent.

"What's krakus ham?" I asked. "Is it from Krakow? Is it Polish for carcass?"

She smiled at me. She spoke English well, but nothing I was saying made sense to her. "Do you want coffee?" she asked.

"Oh, no," I said. "I have insomnia."

She looked at me tenderly. I could have kissed her. She walked away. I imagined her hiding me out during the war years in her barn. She'd bring me krakus ham. We'd make love. I'd survive the war and she and I would come to America and open up the Kiev. I was delirious.

My food came. I ate, and I read the sports section. There was another article on my new hero, Keith Van Horn. I can't help it— I do root for white basketball players. I ate all the pork and found that it was waking me up. All the nitrates in the meat must have been energizing me. I stayed in the Kiev until six-thirty. I paid my bill—it was all of $4.87. I left a dollar tip, like a valentine.

I stepped outside. The sun was up. I was wide awake. I walked down Second Avenue. It wasn't so lovely anymore. Vulturish taxis filled the road. I trudged home. I came in and a cockroach jogged across the floor. I thought of Kafka, which made me think of writing. I sat down at my desk and wrote, "First there was a homosexual fantasy."

A *W* on My *P*

I WAS IN COLLEGE, my sophomore year. A girl I had dated for a while, a sweet girl, came to my dorm room.

"I have venereal warts," she said to me. "I'm supposed to tell you so that you can get yourself checked out."

"Oh, God," I said.

She was sitting on the edge of my bed. This was 1984. We had engaged in a fair amount of condomless sex, which went on quite a bit back then. Nowadays, I don't even like to come on myself. I wear a condom when I masturbate so as not to get something from one of my other personalities. But back in 1984, you didn't wear condoms unless you thought you really had to—like you were deeply concerned about getting the girl pregnant, that sort of easy-going thing. Generally, one did a lot of pulling out, like a retreating army, like Germany from Paris in 1944.

So either I had given the warts to the girl or she possibly had given them to me. I went to the infirmary and got checked out. I didn't have any warts.

She told me about the warts in May, and in August I went to Europe with money I had saved from working as a model, and I wasn't going back to Princeton, I was taking a year off. I traveled extensively, saw most of Europe and Morocco, and then when I was in Switzerland, in mid-October, I saw a little something on my penis. I happened to be on top of an Alp. I then spent a day and a half rushing back down the Alp. I passed a glacier where a James Bond movie was filmed. But who cared? How could I enjoy nature if there was a small piece of skin protruding from my penis? I immediately went to a Swiss hospital. The doctor didn't know what it was. They didn't have warts in Switzerland. It was too clean.

I took a train to Paris. In Paris they knew about warts. I was shown the word for wart in my French-English dictionary. *Verrou.* A nice woman doctor, who looked like the French actress Nathalie Baye, painted my penis with a little brush that she dipped and redipped in a brown liquid. I loved her because she didn't make me feel like a leper. She smiled at me while she painted my penis.

"*Ça va?*" she asked.

"*Oui, ça va,*" I said, and I thought, *Je t'aime.*

All the skin on my penis peeled off that night because of her painting, but at least the wart was gone. And it made my penis look new. It was like a facial.

A few months later, I returned to the U.S., to New Jersey, and I thought I saw the wart again. I was now living at home with my parents, still on my year off. I didn't want to tell my parents about the wart, so I secretly went to a free V.D. clinic in Hackensack on a Friday afternoon. While I waited for the doctor in a little room, I could hear him, through the door, talking to the nurse about the previous patient.

"You should have seen the last guy," he said. "He was loaded with bugs."

Then the doctor came in to see me. He had a large nose that was mottled and Swiss-cheesish from too much drink. His gray hair was unkempt. He was probably an alcoholic, demoted to the V.D. clinic.

I lowered my pants and he looked at my penis: It was extra small the way it is for all officials. He rolled it around in his callused, swollen fingers. I looked at his hairy wrist.

"That's probably a wart," he said. "If I was you, I'd go to a dermatologist. I could put a topical solution on it, but that just removes the skin, it doesn't really kill the wart effectively."

"Is the solution brown?"

"Yes," he said.

"They used that stuff on me in Paris, France."

"You're a lucky young man. I've never been to Paris. I've never been west of Pittsburgh."

His nose was destroyed by alcohol and I was better-traveled, but he had the upper hand: He was a doctor in a V.D. clinic and I was a V.D. sufferer. I had a wart, a tiny little grain of flesh protruding from the middle of my penis. It was no larger than one of those white clouds on my fingernails. I was going to have to find a dermatologist. I drove home from Hackensack and I was depressed and disgusted.

The next morning I felt an itchiness in my crotch. I went in the bathroom and examined myself. There were tiny white formations at the roots of my pubic hairs. They looked like microscopic sacs. I wondered if it was some kind of pubic dandruff. But it was too uniform; the sacs were too consistent, military even. Then I saw a little dark thing, like a spider, embedded in my skin in the middle of my crotch! That doctor had given me crabs! He didn't wash his hands! There must have been a crab in his wrist hair from the patient with the bugs, and the little crab, sensing that it couldn't survive on a wrist for very long, had spotted my crotch and leaped into it for dear life. What did I expect? I had gone to a V.D. clinic and picked up V.D.

I tried to scratch off the tiny crab-spider, but it wouldn't budge. Then I got my fingernail under it good and the thing actually moved in front of my eyes and then redrilled itself into my crotch. I screamed.

My parents were out of the house. It was Saturday and they were away for the weekend.

I called a drugstore in a neighboring town, for reasons of discretion, and a woman answered. I said in a muffled voice, "Do you have anything for lice?"

I thought that lice sounded better than crabs.

"What? What did you ask for?"

"Something for lice, a shampoo." I was still disguising my voice, whispering, though I didn't know her and she didn't know me.

"What *kind* of shampoo?"

I hung up. I called another drugstore in another town. A tough woman with a cigarette voice answered: "Jameson Drugs. How can I help you?"

"Can I speak to the pharmacist?" I asked.

"Maybe I can help you."

"I want to speak to the pharmacist."

"Why?"

Give me the goddamn pharmacist, I wanted to shout. I kept my voice even, but I didn't beat around the bush with this drugstore lady: "I want to speak to the pharmacist because I think I have pubic lice."

"You mean crabs?"

"Yes. Crabs."

I heard her say to the pharmacist, "There's somebody upset on the phone about crabs."

The pharmacist came on with me. "Can I help you?"

I adopted a patrician, Ivy League tone. "I think I might have pubic lice."

"What do they look like?"

"Most of them are extremely tiny and white."

"Attached to the pubic hair?"

"Yes."

"Those are nits. The eggs. They're not actually crabs yet."

"I did see a black spiderlike thing in my skin."

"That's the crab that laid the eggs. You only need one and they lay a thousand eggs. You don't want them to hatch. You better come in right away."

"Will I have to shave my pubic hair?"

He laughed. This wasn't a laughing matter. "No, you don't have to shave," he said. "The shampoo I'll give you comes with a little comb. You comb out the nits."

I drove to the pharmacy. It was a small, old-fashioned place with dusty blow-dryers for sale and weird little gift statues. The store was quiet. There were no other customers. That would make things easier. I walked toward the counter, and I was expecting the cigarette-voiced matron who answered the phone, but there was a young high-school girl. This was her weekend job. I approached her cautiously, pausing to look at toothpaste as if I were a casual shopper. Then I stood in front of her. I tried to spot the pharmacist behind his elevated white wall, but he wasn't there. The girl smiled at me. She was around sixteen. She was a redhead. She had tiny little breasts and her lips were coated with sugary saliva from her chewing gum. I was a monster with crabs and I was attracted to a high schooler.

And I had a venereal wart. A wart that had pursued me from Europe. I had almost forgotten about the wart.

"Can I speak to the pharmacist?"

"Is there something I can help you with?"

The staff of this drugstore were trained to keep people away from the damn pharmacist.

"I really just want to talk to the pharmacist," I said. "I called a little while ago. He told me to come in." The girl smiled at me. I wasn't bad-looking back then. She may have found me attractive. It made being loaded down with two venereal diseases even more upsetting.

"What's your name?" she asked. "I'll get your prescription."

"I didn't give him my name."

"I can find your prescription. What did you call in for?"

I felt faint. I was going to leave. But then an older woman with dyed blond hair came through a door behind the counter. She had just caught the girl's last words, and she looked at my tormented face and she knew who I was. And I knew who she was—the woman who had said *crabs* to me on the phone.

"You're the guy who called," she said with her cigarette voice. "Let me get Bill."

The blonde went back through the private door to get Bill. I was left alone with the cute redheaded teenager. She chewed her gum. I looked at her beautiful, tiny breasts. I thought of high-school boys drinking beer and touching her. I felt itchy and contaminated. I am no longer of this world, I thought.

The cigarette lady came out with the pharmacist, Bill, who was carrying a small box: a box containing pubic lice shampoo. He was a man in his fifties, and he wore a white frock and on his head he had a lacquered-looking, dark-brown toupee, but his unshaved neck hair was gray—he should have at least shaved the mismatched neck hair. Anyway, he nodded at me confidentially and he walked to the far end of the counter so that we could speak quietly. I followed him.

We stopped at a display of pencil eyeliners. He reached out his hand to shake mine. Was he a martyr? Did he want to show that he wasn't afraid of disease? I took his hand. I felt guilty. I didn't tell him that I had caught my crab from a doctor's wrist.

Bill showed me the box and put it down in front of me. "The way you use this stuff is easy," he said. "You put about two capfuls on the nits. You rub it in good. But only leave it ten minutes, otherwise you'll burn yourself. Shower it off with soap. You'll be fine. Then take the little comb that's inside the box and comb the nits out into the toilet. Use the liquid two times a day for the next two days. Everything will be killed off after the second treatment, but do the follow-up just in case."

"All right," I said. The redheaded teenager and the old blonde were to my left, standing at the cash register, and they were silent and I felt that they were secretly listening to Bill prescribe to me the killing of my mother crab and its eggs.

"Also, what's very important," said Bill, "is that you wash all your sheets and towels. And give the house a good vacuuming, too. And wash all your clothes. Use hot water. These things are resilient."

"This is very depressing," I said.

"You're not the first. . . . *I'll* ring you up," he said. He was kind. He understood my embarrassment. I didn't judge him for his toupee.

I was naked in my parents' bathroom and, for good measure, I doubled Bill's prescription: I poured four capfuls on my crotch and I waited twenty minutes. I watched the mother crab pull up her roots. She was less filled with blood now, not so dark-colored, and so she was light blue like a Maryland crab. I screamed again and then I lost track of her in my pubic hair.

I showered for half an hour, and when I was done, I couldn't find the crab. I figured it had been poisoned and then washed down the drain. I had killed the mother and now I was going for her eggs. I removed the metal comb from the box.

I stood over the toilet and I combed out the nits. The metal teeth moved nicely through my pubis, picking up eggs like a leaf rake. And the eggs, little translucent crumbs already loosened by the toxic shampoo, fell easily into the toilet water and hardly made a ripple. The combing was satisfying work: the attention to detail, the repetitive motion, the discovery of a nit I had missed.

I vacuumed the whole house and began an extensive wash. On Sunday afternoon, my parents came home and I was still doing laundry. I was washing towels that hadn't been used in years.

"What's going on?" my mother asked.

I sat both my parents down at the kitchen table.

My mother stayed up the whole night. She rewashed everything.

My parents made only one request of me: I was to use the downstairs toilet. They were afraid of getting crabs and warts from a communal toilet seat. My father asked me, "When are you going back to school?"

I had brought plagues upon my parents' house.

I wasn't able to go to the dermatologist for a few days because I had burned my pubic area with the crab poison. It was very red like a sunburn. I didn't want to go to a doctor for a wart and tell him that I had just gotten over crabs. How much humiliation could I take? I waited for the sunburn to go down.

At the dermatologist's I was put on an examining bed under a special lamp of exceedingly high lumens. The doctor was a very tall, young, prematurely gray-haired man. He was a small-town dermatologist and he said, "I haven't seen a venereal wart since medical school."

To examine me, he put on thick magnifying-lens goggles. He bent his long trunk over and plunged down into the area of my crotch. The goggles made him look like a coal miner.

"You have some redness," he said. The high-intensity lamp had picked up the remaining poison-scalding.

"I was playing tennis in jeans," I said. "It was very chafing."

He found the wart. "It's pretty small," he said. He could have been talking about my penis; it was shrunken and nervous. "But it looks like a wart. I'm going to burn it off. It won't hurt, but the painkiller will."

He took out a four-inch needle of anesthesia. It was six times the size of my penis. The needle gleamed. He sunk it into my penis. I wanted to cry, not so much from the horrible pain, but because of what I was becoming: someone destroyed and mutilated by sex. Then the doctor took a black, pen-sized instrument that had a red tip like a car's cigarette lighter and he burned off my wart.

He bent down very close to take a look after branding me and he said, "This is very embarrassing, but I missed. Your wart is very tiny. But don't worry, the burn heals."

I didn't care. I wasn't going to sue. Cauterize the whole penis, I wanted to tell him. I'll go to a Hasidic shop and buy a wig and start all over. I wanted to be like the Hasidic boy whose penis was snipped off at the age of eight months during a botched repair job on a circumcision. They tried to raise him as a girl, except he didn't take to being a girl. I would take to it. I would marry a Hasid and keep a clean house.

The doctor went at me with the cigarette lighter again and this time he got it. I now had two brown burn marks on my penis. They looked like scorched eyes staring up at me.

A week later the crabs came back. Some little heroic crab egg must have survived in one of my sheets or in my underwear. I called Bill the pharmacist. He said that this was not uncommon.

I went through the whole process again. My mother and I worked together to disinfect our home. We boiled everything. I boiled myself.

At night, during this time, I'd often sit in the downstairs bathroom and I'd study my penis for the wart and my pubic hair for the nits. My mother would grow concerned, and she'd say, "You've been there awhile. Are you all right? Are you sick?"

"I'm fine," I'd say. "Just sitting here thinking."

And my father would say, annoyed, "Leave him alone, he's inspecting the troops."

I had one confidant during this time, a dear friend who had herpes. We determined, and rightly so, that sex was the cause of all our problems. We never wanted to have sex again, nor did we feel we deserved to have sex again. We also swore off masturbation. We'd talk on the phone every night, and we'd inquire as to the other's condition. But the words were so remindful to us of what wretches we had become that we'd only use initials:

"How's your H?" I'd ask.

"All right. How's your W?"

"Fine. Hasn't come back. But there's a hole where it used to be."

"Any C's?"

"No."

"I'll trade you my H for your W and your C's," he'd say. He was always treating our diseases like baseball cards, our old hobby.

"I can't make that trade," I'd say.

"I'll throw in a chlamydia," he'd say. He could use the full word because we'd never had chlamydia, but another friend of ours did have it.

We also used initials if something sexual was to be discussed. We were afraid that a whole word might excite us and we'd break down and think that we should have sex again in our lives. One time he called and said, "I saw a woman with nice B's."

"Oh, no," I said.

"And I came home and I couldn't stop thinking about her B's and I started to M, and then I saw that the H was on my P."

"You finished M'mming?" I asked.

"Yes," he said.

"Did it irritate the H?"

"Yes. My D is destroying my life."

He needed consoling. I said, "Don't worry, I M'mmed, too. I woke up this morning and my P was hard and I thought of this red-headed high-school girl I met and I began to M and then I E'ed."

My friend was silent. I was silent. We were twenty years old and it felt like our lives were over. Then he said, "I really look forward to the day when we can speak in whole words again."

"Me too," I said. "Me too."

For several years after this time of speaking in initials, I was still haunted by the fear that the W or the C's would return. The trauma of it all had been that great. So often when I would visit my parents, I would take refuge in the downstairs bathroom—I hadn't used the upstairs one in some time, out of habit, out of respect—and I'd sit on the toilet and study myself. My parents and I would then play out the same dialogue, over and over. It was sort of a family joke. It amused us.

MOTHER: You've been in there awhile. Are you all right? Are you sick?

ME: I'm fine. Just sitting here thinking.

FATHER: Leave him alone, he's inspecting the troops.

But then around 1990, after a good five years of this, I decided that enough was enough. I was visiting my parents, we had just done our skit, but for me, I knew it was over. This had to stop. I meditated a moment and then a plan came to me. It was not unlike what certain religious groups advocate: I would never look at my penis again. So with courage and conviction I stood up from the toilet, pulled up my underwear, and I haven't looked down since.

II
Problems

Free Meals

I WAS EATING DINNER at Cafe Gitane. I had ravenously gone through most of my Greek salad and then I forked what appeared to be the torn-off end of a used condom. "WHAT'S THIS?" I shouted.

My lovely waitress came over to me. She was Audrey Hepburn–like, which seems to be the way to describe all women who have the beauty of a fragile dark bird. I held up my fork with the shredded rubber and I exclaimed: "I FOUND THIS IN MY FOOD! A TORN CONDOM! I COULD GET PREGNANT! I COULD GET AIDS!" All the Europeans in the café looked at me.

"It's the sanitary glove the cook wears. The finger end," she explained, trying to make sense of it all.

"Did the cook cut off a finger? Maybe I ate the finger. I might have mistaken a fingertip for an olive."

"I'm so sorry," she said.

"I wanted a salad, not finger food. Well, I won't pay for this."

"Of course not. Let me show the manager what happened."

She took my fork and plate and went behind the counter, where a pretty, dark woman was preparing food. She was the cook *and* the manager. She looked at the piece of rubber and then looked at me. She smiled a smile of profound apology. I walked over to the counter.

"You didn't lose a finger, did you?"

"Oh, no," she said. "I'm really embarrassed."

"You don't have TB or hepatitis, do you?"

She laughed. She thought I was joking.

"The salad is on us," she said. "And order anything else you like."

"My appetite is destroyed. . . . Well, I'll have a café au lait and a piece of pie."

I went home. I was feeling pretty good. It's always nice to get a free meal. And emboldened by my good luck at Gitane, I called my parents: I needed an emergency infusion of cash. I was down to thirty-five dollars. They were both on the phone with me and I tried to be brave and ask for the money, but I chickened out. It was too humiliating. But after I hung up I knew that I had no recourse—all my friends had already been tapped.

So I called them back and said, "I have to tell you something—"

But before I could continue, my father said gruffly, "How much?"

I went on with dignity. "I was just wondering if you could pay my health insurance for a few months. A few deals, as you know, haven't come through."

My parents knew that I had been expecting a royalty check from my publisher in Turkey. My first novel is a best-seller over there. It's considered pornographic and indecent, and so it's a great success. I'm the D. H. Lawrence of Istanbul, but I'm broke in New York. My publisher had to seal the book in plastic so that the Turkish children wouldn't read it accidentally, and he claims that legal fees and the cost of the plastic sealing are eating up my royalties.

So my parents kindly agreed to help me, and late the next afternoon, I headed home to get the check. I didn't have time to wait for them to mail it. Just for leaving your apartment in New York, you're charged fifteen dollars.

I took the Path train to Hoboken. I had twenty minutes before my rail connection to northern New Jersey and decided to explore the little port town, which I've never done before. I was hoping to see lots of hobos and find tough bars, but Hoboken has been destroyed: The streets are clean and there is a Barnes and Noble and a Starbucks. And I didn't spot it, but I was sure that a Gap was lurking somewhere nearby. I usually don't care about things like this—the destruction of America—but when I'm traveling, it's nice to find a town with personality.

I was starving, so I went into a deli to buy a sandwich, but even the sandwiches were gentrified. I picked a smoked turkey with sun-dried tomatoes and olive paste. A young counterman with a big nose prepared my sandwich and made a phone call at the same time. With the receiver tucked against his shoulder, he grabbed slices of pale, translucent turkey. And because of the incident at Cafe Gitane, I realized he wasn't wearing rubber gloves.

He nonchalantly touched the phone with his hand and then took that same hand and spread the turkey on my whole wheat. Who had touched the phone before him? It was a daisy chain of germs. And where had his hands been before the phone? Food preparers should wear gloves as if they are taking blood. The whole thing was grotesque. Eating that turkey would be like kissing his fingers. Then he stopped making the sandwich just to talk on the phone.

I thought of skipping out of there. I could run to the station. Then a fat manager-type emerged from the back before I could escape and asked me, "Are you being helped?"

"Yes," I said. "But I do have a train to catch."

I was hoping that this authority figure would then excuse me from having to eat the sandwich, but he scolded his counterman:

"Get off the phone." The kid got off and finished my sandwich. But he forgot the olive paste. I wanted olive paste with the germs.

"Isn't there supposed to be olive paste?"

The manager overheard my question and snarled at the kid, "This sandwich is on me." A free sandwich! My second free meal in two days, but both meals were tainted.

I thought of throwing the sandwich away, but I couldn't—it was free. I got on my train and ate the thing. I tried to be brave, to be like everyone else—people who can eat other people's germs and not care. I finished the sandwich and I stared out the window at the polluted meadowlands.

I felt myself falling asleep; my eyes were closing, and then I thought, Maybe I should just kill myself. Suicidal thoughts always sneak up on me like that. But I don't mind them. They're like aspirin. They calm me down.

My father was waiting for me at the station. We drove home. I felt the old distance, the old repulsion. I fought this. Appreciate him, love him, I told myself.

Whenever I'm with my father, I think of Thornton Wilder's *Our Town* and the scene where the young woman, Emily, who has died in childbirth, gets to leave her grave and go back in time to the day of her twelfth birthday. But it's too painful for her to relive it, and she cries, "I can't. I can't go on. It goes so fast. We don't have time to look at one another."

I played her husband, George, in my high-school production, and I love *Our Town*. I don't care if its brush strokes are broad and sentimental. Its message is good. So I tried to be in the moment with my dad in the car, to *look at him, to be with him.* "How are you?" I asked gently.

"I have a sty in my right eye, and I have numbness in my left foot, but other than that I'm all right."

We were silent for the rest of the car ride. We went home and picked up my mom and headed out for sushi. Before the miso soup arrived, my dad wrote me a check for a couple hundred dollars.

"I should be getting a check from Turkey any day now," I said. "And the new book is coming out in August, in six months. I'll get some more money then."

"We know you're going to make it," said my dad. He has his good moments.

We ate our sushi. It was my third free meal in two days. I thought of telling this to my parents, but my mother also abhors germs, and both the Cafe Gitane and Hoboken stories would have upset her.

They took me to the train station. My mother sat in the back. We waited in the car.

"We support you," my mother said.

"Thank you," I said. "And thank you for the check, and for dinner."

Then the train came. My mother leaned over the front seat and kissed me and said she loved me. I shook my dad's hand and sort of rubbed his shoulder. He smiled at me.

I got out of the car and I leaned in just a little and I said to both of them, "I love you." And then I closed the door.

I took the train back to Hoboken, and then the Path to Ninth Street. From there I walked home and I had an odd pain in my big toe. Something was in my shoe. Whenever this happens, I always remember that in health class in the third grade they showed us a film about a boy who was limping. But then he stopped trying to walk and took off his shoe. Out came a pebble. We were told to always do this if something in our shoe was hurting us—that taking care of one's feet was very important. But I've always been too lazy to empty out the pebbles in my shoes, and this particular night, having gone begging to my parents, I thought I deserved a little suffering.

When I got to my apartment, I took off my shoe and nothing came out. Then I took off my sock and out fell a hard, brown lentil. I hadn't cooked lentils in years. Where had this lentil come from? It was all very strange. Then I thought of all the charity I had received in the last twenty-four hours, so I opened my window and threw the lentil outside. It wasn't much, but I hoped that some poor pigeon might be able to eat it.

Sex in Venice

IN OCTOBER OF 1984, after getting my wart problem taken care of (for the time being, anyway), I settled down in Paris for four months, during which time I had several good adventures. To support myself, I got a job working as an au pair for a French family who lived in Montparnasse. I was given room and board, and I was something of a novelty in the neighborhood—a male nanny. I was referred to as the *au pair garçon Americain,* and it was one of the best jobs I've ever had. My French "mother," whom I spent a great deal of time talking to in the kitchen, was a raven-haired knockout, and early on I stole a pair of her panties in a mad act of affection. They were a faded red with black trim, and I put them on one night and masturbated. Then I threw them away, wanting to destroy the evidence of my crime.

My main task as an au pair was to escort my two children, a girl five and a boy eight, to school each morning, and to pick them up in the afternoon. To get to the school, we took a shortcut through a *boulangerie* on Boulevard de Montparnasse that had a back staircase that led to the road parallel to the boulevard—Rue D'Assas. I was going through a big Hemingway phase then, what with living in Paris, and I read with great glee in *A Moveable Feast* that the man himself cut through the very same bakery on his way to visiting Gertrude Stein. So it was quite exciting as I passed through the delicious-smelling store to think that I was walking in Hemingway's actual footsteps.

In the afternoons, I'd meet my two charges in their school's courtyard, and I always had a snack for them that I had picked up in the Hemingway *boulangerie,* either a *chausson aux pommes* or *pain au chocolat.* So with their pastries in hand, we'd go to the *petit jardin* Luxembourg. They'd meet their friends there and I'd meet with the other au pairs—about a dozen lovely Swedish, Danish, Norwegian, and German girls. The male-female ratio was heavenly, and I quickly took up with a German girl, who was very good at sneaking out of her family's house to visit me (she had some kind of curfew). I, fortunately, had my own room—a *chambre de bonne*—on the eighth floor of my family's building, and around midnight my German would come to me. She would be breathless after climbing so many flights of stairs, and she'd knock at my door and she could barely manage to whisper, but she'd always say, *"C'est moi, c'est moi."*

My room was the size of a large closet. All I had was a mattress on the floor, but it was good for lying down with that sweet girl. She was eighteen, had the tiniest, most adorable little patch of yellow pubic hair, and she loved sex. She would really yell, especially when I mounted her from behind. Her screams made me proud, and my neighbors didn't complain. They were a quiet, mysterious lot—primarily Tunisian and Algerian immigrants, with whom I shared one of those French toilets where you put your feet on these two shoe-sized bricks and you squat over a hole. For someone like myself with toilet neuroses, this kind of toilet is quite excellent—no layering the seat with wads of paper that invariably fall into the bowl as soon as you sit down.

Then Christmastime came and my girlfriend went home, and my French family went to Normandy for two weeks. I was all alone. I stole another pair of panties for some company, but that wasn't enough. So I went out one night to a disco hoping to meet someone, and I managed, after getting quite drunk, to pick up a Danish fashion model. As she and I went to the coat check to leave, a French man got between me and her and he started flirting with the Dane. Liquored up, I told him to back off, that she was with me. He was dark-haired, tall, had a few inches on me, and he shoved me hard in my chest, which surprised me. It knocked me back a foot, and almost without thinking—except for this instantaneous reflexive thought that if another man shoves you, you shove back—I jumped forward and planted my hands on his chest, and I remember thinking that would probably be the end of it, that all I had to do was display one act of not backing down. But right after I shoved him, his fist came out of nowhere and hit me right in the mouth, spinning me around, and my lip split against my teeth. The pain was jarring, but I whirled to face him, without any plan, and he punched me right in the nose, breaking it. It was like a gun had been shot in my face and I saw a bright white light in my eyes.

But then there was red, a blurry rage, and with blood pouring out of my nose like warm water, I managed to tackle the guy, but not bring him down. I had him in a sort of headlock, and I couldn't hear anything, the world was silent, but I saw the Dane with her mouth open, screaming obviously, and everyone was backing away, leaning against the walls, frightened yet forming a natural voyeuristic ring. As I held him with my right arm (and I was a pretty strong kid from years of sports, so he couldn't break loose), I tried to throw two lefts up into his chin. I vaguely remembered Hemingway writing somewhere that in a fight you should throw two left uppercuts and one right cross. Well, one of my lefts landed without much power, one glanced off his shoulder, and then I loosed my right arm from around his neck and threw a wild haymaker punch, my cross, which missed completely. And the force of my failed blow had me partially bent over in front of the guy and he took my head in his hands like a punter with a football and he brought his knee up and I managed to turn so his kneecap didn't crash into my face but the side of my skull. This sent me flying. It was like being hit with a bat. There was no white light this time, but a temporary painful blackness. And this blow with the knee spun me around just like the first punch had, and when I came out of the blackness, my back was to him. He's killing me, I thought, and I knew I was beaten, but I wasn't going to quit. Something asserted itself in me, some vain, noble, nihilistic pride, and I turned to face him, expecting in my defenseless state to be hit again. But several bouncers had him now, they had perceived that he was the bad guy, probably because he was killing me, and they threw him out. And the Dane was gone. Everyone was looking at me. A bouncer gave me a towel for my nose; he asked me if I was all right, and I said for everyone to hear, *"Ça fait rien."* It means nothing.

Then about a half hour later when I was alone in my little room, I cried. I felt this weird fear and sadness and aloneness about having been beaten up. I had a split lip, a cut on my head, and weird purple swelling on the bridge of my nose.

About a week after the fight, it was Christmas Eve, and with my face having rather quickly healed, except for my nose, which was still tender and somewhat purple, I decided to do some traveling to cheer myself up and I bought a train ticket to Venice. I made my choice because of Thomas Mann's *Death in Venice*. Most of my youthful travels were inspired by literature—Berlin: Isherwood; Spain and Paris: Hemingway; Morocco: Bowles; and the Côte d'Azur: Fitzgerald.

I arrived in Venice on Christmas morning. Almost all the hotels were shut down until the new year, and the few that were open were booked. But I did manage to get an unheated room on the top floor of a small hotel. The room was only used in the summer, but the manager took pity on me and let me have it, which I was very grateful for, because otherwise I had nowhere else to go. He gave me extra blankets and it was extremely cold in Venice, but I slept with my clothes on and my winter coat, and it was somehow manageable.

So I spent my days wandering around the freezing, empty city. I hardly saw other people. Everyone was hiding. I took a water-bus to Lido and looked for Thomas Mann but didn't find him either. In all my book-inspired traveling, I would madly go looking for the writers I loved, somehow hoping to find them, as if they would come back to life just for me.

What else can I say about Venice? It was gray, sad, and otherworldly. It was the most beautiful place I had ever been. I swore to myself that I'd return someday with someone I loved.

At night there were a few restaurants open and I would drink a lot of wine, and one night after dinner and a bottle of wine, I went to the famous Harry's Bar. I drank several gin and tonics because the bartender told me that's what Harry's was famous for. The drinks were incredibly overpriced—I didn't realize this when I started—and I just about emptied out my wallet. I left the bar angry and feeling ripped off, but the cold air calmed me down and I went walking along the water, the open sea, near Piazza San Marco. I stopped at a railing just to look out and to listen to the water, and an old man suddenly slipped alongside me and scared me. I hadn't heard him approach. He saw I was startled. He said something. "No Italiano," I said. He knew enough English to say, "I want to kiss you." He made a hand-motion toward my fly.

"No, *grazie,*" I said.

"Please," he said. He was tiny, bald, wearing a nice coat. His eyes were not unkind. "Please."

"*Si,*" I said. I was speaking Italian and he was speaking English.

I was drunk, but I knew what I was doing. He led me to a little, partially enclosed dock so that no one could see us. He knelt down and he was smiling beautifully. I unzipped. For once it was to my advantage to come quickly, but it took me forever. But eventually, standing on that freezing-cold dock, I did come. I helped the old man stand up and I got out of there.

I walked back to my hotel. I took a scalding-hot shower in the bathroom down the hall, trying to pretend to myself that I hadn't done what I'd done, and then I got back into my clothes and my winter coat—my Venice pajamas in my unheated room. I lay in bed, but I couldn't sleep. I saw the old man in my mind getting down on his knees. I saw how happily he smiled. Maybe it wasn't a bad thing. I had come to this city looking for *Death in Venice* and Thomas Mann, and in my own way I had sort of found both.

The Young Author

I WAS WALKING DOWN A HANDSOME, brownstonish street in Brooklyn Heights and I came upon a fresh box of Q-Tips. It was a nice-looking box—very blue. And it was still sealed in plastic. I need Q-Tips, I thought. I picked up the box and looked around. There were no other pedestrians within fifty yards. I sort of waved the box in the air to signal to the world that I was willing to give the Q-Tips back to their rightful owner. No one claimed them. What a strange item to have fallen out of someone's bag.

I checked the seal thoroughly. It was perfect. And it seemed unlikely that the little sticks with their heads of cotton could be contaminated in any way, though I did imagine, for a moment, a madman dipping the Q-Tips in some kind of poison and then resealing the box and planting it on the sidewalk. He could be watching me at that very moment. But this was too preposterous. I pocketed the Q-Tips and headed back to Manhattan. I had wanted Q-Tips for some time. But it was a luxury item—I only spend my money on the most necessary goods.

My unexpected find came in handy a few days later. The publisher of my novel, due out in five months, was taking me to lunch at the "21" Club. And the morning of the lunch, I did a thorough cleaning of myself, and I employed several Q-Tips. I wanted to look very good for the lunch; I prepared for it like an actor, because often when I meet people whom I have to impress, my personality is mysteriously vacuumed away. I become as boring as a piece of toast. But if I try to play a role, if I try to be someone other than myself, I can sometimes make a good impression. And so for my luncheon at "21," where there were going to be several people whom I had never met, I geared myself up to play the Young Author. It's what I did eight and a half years ago when I prematurely ejaculated my first book at the age of twenty-five. But at thirty-three I can still be the Young Author; the window doesn't close on that title for another two years.

The first step in my transformation was a bath and a shave. I also washed my hair and worked on my scalp with my rubber invigorator. I then used the invigorator on the soles of my feet to give myself some amateur reflexology.

After the bath, I put sunscreen on my face to act as a moisturizer. Then I put a little dab of wheat germ oil in the palm of my hand and with some water rubbed this into my hair. I then combed back my front fringe of hair over my bald spot. The wheat germ oil held the hair in place quite nicely and gave me a wet look— very good for Young Authors striving for an allusion to Fitzgerald.

Then I opened up my beautiful box of new Q-Tips. I again thought of the mad poisoner, but only for a second. I dipped a Q-Tip into my bottle of hydrogen peroxide (a very cheap thing, peroxide, only eighty-nine cents for a good-sized bottle, and it has so many uses) and I cleaned my ears. I did this very gently, because I have a great fear of puncturing the eardrum ever since I read some years ago that some baseball player had done just that with a Q-Tip while sitting in the dugout.

Then I gargled with the peroxide and hot water—it gets rid of germs and cleans up coffee stains. I followed up the gargling with flossing, and then a gentle brushing of my teeth because my gums are receding like my hair.

I was almost ready to get dressed, but then I inspected myself closely in the mirror—there were three long blond hairs coming out of my nostrils and several hairs out of both ears. I once had a small nostril-hair scissor, but unfortunately I lost it on a visit to New Hampshire in 1990, and I've been too cheap ever since to get a new one. So I tried trimming the nostril hairs with my nail-clipper, but it didn't work. I then tried getting my razor in my nose and almost cut in half the little wall that exists between the two nostrils. So I took some wheat germ oil and glued the nostril hairs to the inside of my nose.

I then tried cutting the ear hairs with the nail-clipper—even though it didn't work on the nose hairs—and, naturally, I was unsuccessful, but I did manage to cut this little piece of cartilage at the front of my right ear. Blood was drawn. At this point I thought I was starting to overdo things, and sensed that if I didn't stop myself, I might destroy my face as a way to sabotage my luncheon and my whole career.

So I headed for the closet and removed my clothes. A few days earlier a benefactor of mine, an older writer, had taken me to Brooks Brothers. I don't have any money left from my book advance, spent all of it in '97, so my benefactor bought for me a beautiful charcoal-gray herringbone sport coat. This way I would have something good to wear for the lunch. The plan is for me to pay him back for the coat by doing copy-editing work on his latest opus.

I got dressed and tied my tie perfectly the first attempt—a good sign, I thought. Then I put on my splendid herringbone, and to affect an Edwardian appearance—to go with my thinning, red-blond hair and blue eyes—I fastened all three buttons. I thought to myself, I almost look like a real person.

I often don't feel like a real person because my existence is dominated by fear. It keeps me from feeling alive. I am like a Q-Tip—my body is this stick that walks around attached to a head that is a cotton swab of anxiety. But I think that people who wear herringbone sport jackets must not be so fearful. They're in charge of themselves. And putting on my herringbone really helped me get into my role of the Young Author. In fact, I was a Confident Young Author. My sport coat was like a WASPy, Edwardian suit of armor. But the *herring*bone part makes it Jewish, so it's perfect for me: WASPy in appearance, Jewish in spirit. In fact, I'm wearing my jacket right now to elevate my mood as I sit here at my wobbly desk. Even in the privacy of my own home, I often don WASP attire. I call this religious cross-dressing.

So my whole toilet and costuming had taken almost two hours, but I had about forty-five minutes to kill before getting on the subway, so I studied my book of Oscar Wilde epigrams. I was hoping to use one or two during the luncheon conversation. Then promptly at noon, I sheathed myself in my Barracuda raincoat and headed out.

When I was on the street, I found it to be an unusually mild February day, and it was also a little rainy, and as I walked to the F train, a man approached me and he sneezed convulsively twice in succession. And because it was so misty and drizzly, I could see the particles of his sneeze in the moisture—the way you can see dust in a sunbeam. The sneeze-motes spread out from his body a good three yards, and I was in their line of fire. I astutely jumped into the road to avoid contamination, but I was sure that some of the germs had gotten to me, and I was worried that I'd be sick by the time I got to the restaurant. Shaken, I continued on to the subway, and I did feel some concern that I was perhaps growing more and more insane on this issue of germs.

Without further incident, and no sense of sore throat or any other symptoms of contagion, I made it to "21," which is in this tiny, old building stuck between two skyscrapers. I went inside and the place is very much in the style of an old-fashioned men's club— dark wood, low ceilings, deferential staff.

I deposited my raincoat and then went into the bathroom to make sure that the wheat germ oil had my hair in place. I did a little combing and then I washed my hands, since I had been on the subway. Some fears of germs are more rational than others.

When I approached the maître d', he told me that my party had yet to arrive, so I waited at the bar and had a Pellegrino. I wished I could have a drink and let the booze substitute for my personality, but there was no telling what I might pull since I suffer from dipsomania.

Then the people from the publishing house arrived and they were all glad to see me, but I immediately began to bore them. I was as dry as toast. I just kept nodding and smiling, but secretly my mind was polluted with thoughts about my lunch companions in their most private moments wiping their asses. Why did I have to produce such alienating daydreams? These were the people who would be making decisions about my book—the cover, the marketing, the advertising. How could I maintain a facade of grace and intelligence when my mind was boiling like a scatologically crazed mental patient? My dark side was obviously trying to undermine me. I could feel the suspicions of my lunch companions growing— *He couldn't possibly have written that book, maybe it's not as good as we think.* I was losing them for sure, but then I looked down at my sport coat and I rallied. The herringbone took over and I became the Young Author. I was witty, charming, complimentary. I had delicious Chilean sea bass, and in response to the fish, I quoted Wilde on the virtues of pleasure. They all beamed at me, seemed to like me. So the whole lunch turned out to be rather perfect: I wasn't myself and the food was free.

Enemas: A Love Story

SEVERAL MONTHS AFTER the *Press* published my story about the late arrival of my puberty, a reader was still moved enough to write to me care of the paper. The letter arrived in an envelope made of very good stock, but there was no return address. The letter itself was handwritten with almost calligraphic beauty and was on very nice stationery. But its simple message was only one sentence long. It read as follows: "Mr. Ames, you should follow up your puberty article with one about your enema experiences."

The letter was signed by a Joseph Gitcha. I assume that this is a false name, and that the purpose of the letter was to criticize my choice of subject matter, but as I read the letter I considered Joseph's suggestion. I thought to myself that my experiences with enemas *would be* a good theme for an article. I've covered colonics, but not enemas, and there *is* a difference. Thus, I've written down here what I know, and so Joseph Gitcha, wherever you are, whomever you are, this is for you.

During the summer of 1985, I was a camp counselor in Vermont at a place called Camp Thoreau. One night in early August, I went out with my fellow Thoreau counselors to a bar. I got drunk and I ate a rancid sandwich and the next day I came down with a fever and a severe case of diarrhea that lasted for ten days. The timing was excellent: I didn't have to go on the big canoe trip with my boys and I was allowed to lay on my bunk and just read. I'd glance out the window to the Vermont firs and I hoped the diarrhea would last the rest of the summer so that I didn't have to spend any more time pitching softballs and making thirteen-year-old boys line up and be quiet.

But then some blood started appearing in my stool and they tested it for microorganisms, like salmonella, but there were none. So the camp doctor took me to Dartmouth Hospital. The doctor there, a proctologist, was concerned that I might have colon cancer. He was a clean-looking man with a pink, sunburned bald spot. The kind of burnt bald spot that looks obscene and cancerous. He was worried that I had colon cancer, and I was worried that he had skin cancer. I wanted to tell him to use sun-block, but I didn't think it was my place.

So I was upset about this colon scare, but I had often received ominous diagnoses in my life. When I was born, I was jaundiced and I was placed upside down in a special container to drain the bile from my liver. When I was eight, I had my lower-back spasms and my ascended left testicle problem.

Then when I was nine, I fell out of a tree from a great height and my head was at such a strange angle that a neighbor yelled at me not to move. The ambulance came and I was put on a stretcher as if my neck had been broken. It turned out to be only a severe sprain, but my head was still at an unusual tilt: I walked around for a few days with my ear almost touching my shoulder. So I was taken to a chiropractor. His method with children, since they were prone to squirming, was to leave the room and come in another door and sneak up from behind the child, grab its chin in his powerful hands, and snap its neck. He did this to me and I screamed and I looked at my mother, whose eyes pleaded with me for for-giveness. She had been privy, I realized, to his sneaky plan. But I forgave her. I always forgave my mother, and my head was back to normal and that felt good.

Then shortly after I almost broke my neck, I noticed that my troublesome left testicle had descended. My father opined that my fall from the tree had dislodged it. He was very happy about saving the money on the testicle surgery.

"The chiropractor cost a lot," he said, "but surgery on your ball would have been a lot more."

Another medical crisis occurred when I was sixteen and I was picking my nose so deeply and aggressively while watching televi-sion that I punctured a vein. I didn't realize this, but I knew the bleeding was heavy. I went and hid in my room and I wrapped a towel around my head and nose like a tourniquet. I had caused many nosebleeds from nose-picking, and I didn't want my family to know that I had done it yet again. But when the bleeding didn't stop after an hour and a half, I went down to the kitchen. Blood was soaking through the towel and onto the floor, and I said to my mother, "I banged my nose against the door and it seems to be bleeding very heavily."

My sister, sitting at the kitchen table, said, "You were picking your nose again, weren't you?!"

Turns out I was hemorrhaging from the nostril and I had to be rushed to the emergency room. The doctor there cauterized the vein I had punctured with my fingernail. He said if I had let the bleeding go another half an hour, I might have died. Death from nose-picking. I had to wear a white bandage around my nose for the next two weeks. It was sort of like a nasal eye-patch. There was a family wedding during this time of my nose-patch and I wasn't allowed in any of the photos.

Then there was the medical catastrophe that occurred when I went abroad for the first time. I was nineteen and met up with my Princeton girlfriend, Claudia, in Vichy, France. We wanted to take the waters. She went out one afternoon and I read her diary. I chanced upon a description of an affair she'd had two months earlier in Colorado Springs, the site of the Olympic Training Center. She made a point of commenting in her journal that the fellow's penis was much larger than my own. My only consolation was that he was an Olympic athlete. Of course I was smaller than an Olympian.

I would have left her, but I started having an extraordinary headache soon after reading the diary and I wasn't able to travel, to escape. I didn't tell her what I had read. I thought on the second day of the headache that a good lunch might set me straight. I was alone, the cheating girlfriend was off sight-seeing, and I went to a restaurant. I didn't understand the menu, and when they brought out my entree, it was a small grilled sparrow. Its head was intact and lay on the plate at a rakish angle. It was like my head when I fell from the tree. I felt a tremendous empathy for that little bird. It reminded me of the little brown birds I grew up with in New Jersey, and then I suddenly missed New Jersey and my mother. The pain in my head expanded. I thought of the Olympian's penis. I collapsed at the table.

I came to in Vichy Hospital. I was running a fever of 104. The strange pressure in my head was incredible. I was crying constantly for painkillers. For two days they thought I had a brain tumor. They X-rayed me quite a lot. I was brave and I didn't call my parents.

Then an American doctor came and diagnosed me as having a severe case of sinusitis. I was ecstatic not to have a tumor. I was put on antibiotics and the headache went away. But I spent ten days in the hospital and I grew a little beard. They gave me a robe to wear with pockets. I kept chocolate in the pockets and I pretended that I was a wounded American soldier. My temperature was taken rectally each morning at six-thirty A.M. I fell in love with my nurse who administered the thermometer. She had dark, black hair and beautiful, puffy French lips. She'd pull back my blanket and I'd lift my hips. I made bedroom eyes at her whenever she slipped it to me.

My girlfriend came to visit and I didn't tell her I had read her diary, but I broke up with her. I told her that I had fallen in love with my nurse.

So my liver, my testicle, my neck, my nose, and my brain had all been on the verge of collapse at different times in my life, and there I was at twenty-one in the Dartmouth Hospital being informed that now my colon was in danger. The proctologist explained to me that he was going to put a rubber telescope up my rectum, but before he could do that, I had to be given enemas. He wanted my colon to be clean so that he could see what was happening up there.

I was to be given three enemas over the course of one hour. I was put in a room with a toilet. My nurse was a no-nonsense lady with yellow hair and the figure of a good, country Vermont mother. She handed me the first of my three enemas. It was a little plastic tube filled with liquid. It was the size of a water-dropper for a pet in a cage. The tip of the tube was plugged with foil. She told me that I could administer the enema myself, in private. I was to lie on the table, legs in the air, and squirt into myself the contents of the plastic dropper. Once it was administered, I was to go and sit on the toilet and wait.

"I'll be back in twenty minutes with your next one," she said. "Don't forget to peel off the foil."

I followed her orders and went and sat on the toilet. I thought it wasn't working. For some reason this gave me a sense of superiority—that I was an unusual person who didn't respond to enemas. Then a pressure hit my bowels as if a cold ocean wave had been released.

"My God!" I exclaimed. I thought I would explode, but not from the anus. I thought my intestine was going to burst out and unfurl from my gut like a wild snake. Then I did explode from the usual channel. There was a great burning sensation. After it was over, I remained on the toilet, my head in my hands. The yellow-haired nurse knocked on the door. I pulled up my underwear. She handed me my next dropper. I closed the door and shot myself in the ass.

Twenty minutes later she was back. She was stony-faced, unsympathetic. By the third enema, I was exhausted and ready to confess.

She took me to a fancy examining room. I was put on my side on a table and I was draped with a paper gown. Another nurse took over. She was a white-haired angel.

"I'll be with you through the whole thing," she said. "If you want to cry, that's all right."

"Thank you," I said. I didn't know exactly what she was talking about. I was still reeling from the enemas. Then the proctologist came in with a woman and two men.

"How you doing?" the proctologist asked.

"All right," I said. The kindly nurse wheeled a cart with a large tray alongside me. On top of the tray, coiled like a garden hose, was a thick black tube. It had the width of a policeman's club. The doctor explained that this hose was the telescope he had told me about earlier. It had a camera and a magnifying lens and he was going to take a look inside me and see what was causing all this bleeding. He also said that there were little pincers at the end of the tube and he was going to do a biopsy, but that I wouldn't feel a thing. The sweet nurse held my hand while all this was explained.

The doctor prepared me with some cold lubricant, which felt soothing after the enemas, and then he asked, "Is it all right if these students take a look with me?"

He was referring to the woman and the two men. I wanted to be helpful. I gave my permission. It was a way to flirt with the female student. She was comely; she had dark, sympathetic eyes. I hoped that she would pity me and like me. I thought of my nurse in Vichy and the rectal thermometer.

The doctor began to insert the tube and the old white-haired nurse squeezed my hand tightly.

"You're very brave," she said. "Try to breathe."

She was treating me like I was a sacrificial virgin, and I was concerned how painlessly the tube was going in. I didn't want the nurse to think that I was used to such large objects having their way with me. But in high school I had put my hairbrush handle up my rear after I read about someone doing that in *Penthouse.* I had enjoyed the hairbrush handle, it struck some unknown nerve, and I had abused it several times. As a curse, I am now balding and soon will have no need of hairbrushes.

The telescope was uncoiled into me and I felt nothing. I took it like a car being siphoned of gas. But I closed my eyes for the sweet nurse as if I was in pain and I moaned and I winced.

"You poor dear," she said. "Breathe, and it will be all right."

I moaned again. I tried to produce a tear. I didn't want her kindness to be wasted on someone whose ass was so easily ravaged.

"Don't worry," said the proctologist. "You'll get used to it and the pain will stop."

Finally, it was all the way up there and the doctor passed the viewing end around to the students and they all enjoyed looking inside me and made small, clucking student-noises of appreciation. I tried to glance at the pretty woman student to see her reaction, to see if she liked my colon, but the doctor told me to be still. Then he studied things himself for a little while.

When he was finished, he said, "Do you want to take a look?"

"All right," I said. He passed me the viewing end of the hose and I peered in and I saw a large pink, ribbed tunnel. It was glossy and nice-looking.

"I see a tunnel," I said.

"That's your colon," he said.

Suddenly there was a stream of water coming right at my eye. I instinctively pulled back from the lens, and then the water passed by the camera. "I just saw some fluid!" I said with alarm, thinking that I might have witnessed something intended for the doctor's eyes.

"That's only the saline fluid from the enema," he said.

I was shocked that there was any left. I thought I had been completely drained, and it was interesting that I could see the fluid but not feel it. I peered at myself for another few seconds. I had recently been thinking about the mind/body problem in philosophy, and while looking at my colon, I suddenly experienced déjà vu. There was a profound sense of familiarity. It felt like a great discovery. I said to the doctor, to the room at large, "I feel that I've seen this before. That I know it perfectly."

No one said anything and they took the viewer away from me. As the tube was being removed, I said to the sweet nurse, who was holding my hand again, "My mind must have a blueprint of every organ in my body. A map. A guide. The mind and body are one."

"You're very brave," she said. "Most people complain the whole time." She was trying to be kind. She thought I was delirious with pain and speaking nonsense.

I was returned to my room and I kept thinking about what a nice pink colon I had, how enjoyable it had been to look at. I stared down at my underwear and it was nice to know that my colon was in there. I felt like I had an ally inside me, and I experienced a love for my body that I had never known before. I loved all the crazy parts of me, no matter how rebellious they became, no matter how many false alarms they rang, no matter how many hospitals they landed me in. I was one with all my parts. I was one with my body.

I left the hospital and a few days later I was told that there was no cancer. Then they retested my stool and it was discovered that I did have a microorganism, not unlike salmonella, but more rare. I went on antibiotics and the whole thing cleared up.

So I thank you, Joseph Gitcha. Your letter came at a good time: I had forgotten about my enema experience; I had forgotten about my breakthrough with the mind/body problem. And recently I had become very angry with my body. I was obsessing about the constant bloating that I was having in the area above the pubis. I couldn't get any work or writing done. I kept looking at my bloating. Day after day it wouldn't go down, and I don't have enough money to get another colonic. I'm broke, living on a shoestring. So I fasted, ate only fruit, and prayed. I took extra doses of psyllium, a fiber supplement that I enjoy. But I was like a blowfish unable to deflate. I was infuriated with my colon, at how poorly it digested everything. And then your letter came and reminded me that I had once felt very good about my colon. I knew what to do. I went out and bought an enema after reading your note. I wanted to feel one with my body again. The directions on the enema box recommended doggy-style. There was a drawing. But I thought it was best to re-create the events of 1985 in Vermont when I had done it in the missionary position.

So I lay on the floor and shot myself in the ass, and when I was done in the bathroom, I felt light and good and I wrote this piece.

A Literary Battle

I DON'T LIKE THIS STRANGE, hot March weather. The East Village is like a college campus and all the coeds are prematurely running around braless and showing a lot of leg. I'm not ready yet to exchange my winter depression for warm-weather sexual titillation. I'm gawking so much that I'm likely not to look where I'm going and I'll step in a sewer hole and twist an ankle. There is so much good ass out there. But I wonder, Who's sleeping with these girls? Not me. Not my friends. I just walk up and down Second Avenue and shamelessly rubberneck with my pencil neck, which makes me a rubber pencil neck.

I want snow. I don't want to have to look at girls. Two winters ago there was plenty of snow. I was holed up in Brooklyn and only had to go out once in a while to teach grammar at the business school in Manhattan that was good enough to employ me. But often classes were canceled because of the weather. So I spent most of my time in my little apartment, which was right next to the Brooklyn-Queens Expressway. I'd sit at my desk and try to write my novel. But it was difficult working there. Whenever a truck would rumble by on the highway, the whole little building would shake. I felt seasick the entire two years I was living there.

So this seasickness gave me a good excuse to abandon the desk and lie on my futon and masturbate. Because of the seasickness, I pretended I was a sailor, and this helped rationalize all the masturbation, because a real sailor who worked on a Greek tanker once told me that a sailor's life consisted of three things: rust, sperm, and beer. They spent all day battling rust—chipping it off and painting over it—and in their free time they jerked off and drank beer. Sailors are adventurous, romantic figures, so I was glad to think of myself as one, to qualify as one, since I was such a wanker in my little tanker of an apartment.

Sometimes, though, when I masturbated, I wanted company. But the snowdrifts were enormous outside and made leaving my house too daunting a task. So I took solace in phone sex. But because I was broke and cheap, I would call this fifteen-cents-a-minute homosexual line. All the heterosexual lines were much more expensive. This is where it's handy to be polymorphously perverse—you can save money.

So I would call the sex line, and it was some kind of telephonic bulletin board for men seeking sexual partners. And I liked hearing all the wacky messages. There were so many desperate people out there that I felt less alone.

Then one time I discovered that on this bulletin board line there was a *live* option, which I hadn't realized. I checked it out and I started talking to this fellow, and after some basic introductions—our names (I gave a false one: Jim), appearances, and penis lengths (I added an inch)—he said to me, "Are you into chicken fights?" He had a thick Bay Ridge accent.

"You mean illegal cock fighting?" I asked. I thought he might be into such an activity because of the word *cock*.

"No, chicken fights. You know, where one guy gets on the shoulders of another guy. You into that?"

"Well, I haven't done it for many years," I said.

"It's what I like to do. We could get together and I'll climb on your shoulders, naked."

"But who would we fight?"

"Nobody, but you could carry me around," he said, quite earnestly in his rough Bay Ridge tones. "We could practice, and then in the summer we could go to Jones Beach and have chicken fights with other guys."

He had really thought this out; it was a strange, sad little fantasy. I figured that as a boy he must have been having chicken fights and got an erection while straddling the neck of a good friend, but had been unable or too embarrassed to articulate to his pal what had happened. So who knows for how many years he had been fruitlessly trying to recapture that moment.

I thought I should try to help illuminate my phone partner. Perhaps if he contemplated the origins of his fantasy, he wouldn't be so ruled by it, which seemed to be the case. "You must have had a good experience with chicken fights as a boy," I said, like a therapist.

"No," he said angrily. "It's a fun thing to do now. It's like foreplay. You've just never tried it." And then the line was dead. He wanted sex, not therapy, for which I don't blame him.

A few days after the chicken-fight conversation, I was listening again to the bulletin board and one message was very intriguing. This man wanted to get together in a hotel room and box while only suited up in underwear. This sounded more reasonable than shadow chicken fighting, and though I had never called anyone from the bulletin board—much to my amazement, the men gave out their home phone numbers—I wanted to call this boxing enthusiast. I happen to have a great interest in boxing. I studied it in 1992 at the Kingsway Gym on Fortieth Street. At the time, I thought I might want to write about boxing, *and* I had a great desire to be in a fight. To be hit and yet keep standing. To strike a perfect blow. But I only trained for one month, and to be allowed to spar at Kingsway, you had to be a member for three months. So for several years after my boxing lessons, I still had a hankering to apply the Queensberry rules to someone's chin. I called the man on the bulletin board.

"Hello," he answered in a gruff voice.

"I heard your message on the bulletin board."

"You like to box?"

"Yeah," I said, matching his gruff, conspiratorial tone.

"What do you do for a living?" he asked. He probably was hoping to tangle with a construction worker, something rugged.

"I'm a writer," I said.

"Me too," he said, and after that our voices became much less rough and more articulate. We talked about the loneliness of a writer's life, the constant struggle, though at that moment his career was on an upswing. He had a nonfiction book coming out in a few months with a reputable publisher. It occurred to me that he might be a good contact. I was networking on a homosexual phone-sex line.

"I'm writing a novel," I said. "But it's going slowly."

"Maybe you need a break," he said. "Let's get a room at the St. Mark's Hotel and box. It will loosen you up. I have gloves and headgear."

Offers like this don't come about too often, and an hour later, I met him in front of the hotel. He was standing with one foot on a snowbank. He was a tall, rangy man in his early forties with a handlebar mustache. He had a duffel bag filled with the boxing gear. We shook hands and I felt shy, but not too shy—I was with a fellow writer. He rented the room and I didn't offer to split the cost; he was the one with a book coming out.

Our boxing suite was tiny and narrow, hardly an official-sized ring. Following his instructions, we stripped down to our underwear, laced on our gloves, and strapped on our headpieces. Then he said, "Whoever gives up first has to suck the other one's cock."

He hadn't mentioned this over the phone. And I had been naive to think that he would only want to engage in fisticuffs. But this notion of cocksucking didn't appeal to me at all. Even though he was a writer, that handlebar mustache gave him a dirty look, which to my germ-sensitive worldview was not appealing.

"I'm really just into the boxing," I said diplomatically.

He was disappointed, but then we began. I think he was hoping to beat me into submission, into cocksucking. Suddenly the fight took on grave consequences.

He crowded in and started off with body blows, which I deflected with my elbows. But then he began pounding me on the side of the head and pushing me around. I was in shock. I was in a fight in a hotel room. What was I doing? How did I end up here? He caught me in the stomach, winded me. If this kept up, I was going to have to suck a cock. I was in danger. I should have met up with the chicken-fight guy.

He backed me into the corner by the door. My gloves were protecting my face. He caught me on the side of my headgear. It made my head ring, but it woke me up. Fight back, Ames! Show some spirit. I pushed him off me so that I could fire my jab. I threw two quick jabs in succession, which he blocked, but I followed the jabs, as I had been trained at Kingsway, with a blow to his stomach and I got him good. And I felt good. His eyes narrowed with pain and surprise. Maybe my mouth wasn't going to get sodomized. I threw two more jabs rapidly, which he blocked, but that was my plan—I then threw a lightning bolt of a right cross that caught him in the side of the head and he went tumbling onto the hotel bed. Maybe I'd make him suck *my* cock, though I didn't like that mustache.

He got back up and charged me and pushed me against the wall. He tried to rub his underwear against me a little, and he threw an unskilled tantrum of punches into my rib cage. I let him have his fun and then I pushed him off me and did a quick one-two and caught him again with a cross on the side of the head. And my blow was so fierce that it knocked off his headgear and sent him stumbling backward, and he gouged his hip on the corner of the bureau, screamed, and fell to the bed in genuine agony.

Our tiny little boxing ring had worked against him, and I felt terrible about his hip. He was in the kind of pain where you stub your toe and you wish, momentarily, that life would end. He lay there clutching his wounded side, his face tormented. "Are you all right?" I asked.

"I think we better stop," he said in a pained whisper. "We don't have good chemistry." Chemistry? It was a first-round knockout.

I got dressed and he just lay there on the bed. I felt bad seeing him defeated, his dream of victory and a blowjob destroyed. But sometimes I have to look after myself. "Good luck with your book," I said as I opened the door to leave.

"Good luck with yours," he said. And so we parted amicably— two writers wishing each other well.

I Was a Son, I Was a Father

IN 1988, MY PARENTS almost died, I met my son, and I finished my first novel.

Some things happened in 1987 that contributed to 1988. In June of '87, I graduated from Princeton. A few days after graduation, I received a book contract for a novella I had written during my senior year. The contract stipulated that I was to expand the novella into a full-length novel by December of 1987. This was a dream come true—I was going to be a published writer. I moved to New York City to write my book.

In July of 1987, I received a letter from a woman whom I hadn't spoken to in two years. She was someone I had slept with once. She was quite a bit older than me, thirteen years. She lived in Georgia, but we met in Vermont the summer I was a camp counselor. She taught music at the camp and one night we got a little tipsy and I was alone with her in her cabin. And a bat flew in the window. We both screamed. It was flying around madly, and I said, "I don't think bats can see in the light." I said this out of some vague recollection that bats are blind, so I turned out the light and we waited, afraid, scared, and then I turned the light back on and the bat was gone. I said proudly, feeling like a real outdoorsman, "See, I was right," and as soon I said that, the bat flew right between us, like some kind of blind-bat cupid, and once more we screamed. I turned the lights out again and put my arm through hers, to protect her, for protection, and the touch led to another, and then we were on her bed—the lights never came back on—and we made love. The next day, she felt embarrassed because I was so much younger, and we never did it again. And when camp ended, I never thought I'd see her again.

So two years later, she wrote me this letter and with it was a picture of a fifteen-month-old baby boy with red hair and blue eyes. My red hair and blue eyes. She wrote that I was the father of this child, and she said she was sorry for not writing me sooner, but she knew I was in college and she didn't want to burden me, but that as time went on, she realized I had the right to know. She made no demands of me. She said I could do whatever I wanted to do, meet him or not meet him, but that she just wanted me to know. It was a simple, beautiful letter, and I held the picture of this red-haired baby. I knew he was my son and I wanted to see him.

But I've always been the kind of person who can tackle only one problem at a time. And the first problem, in my mind, was the book. I figured I could finish it in a month, two months at the most. After all, I had written the first half in eight months—while taking classes. Without classes, it would have to go quickly. Then when the book was done I could go see my son.

I wasn't able to write at all. In September I moved back to Princeton, thinking that New York was the problem. I rented a small room in a house with some graduate students. At the end of October the stress of everything led to a week-long drinking binge and then a month-long hospitalization.

By January of 1988, I still hadn't written a word. And I hadn't gone to see my son. I couldn't go see him, in my mind, until the book was done. It's not entirely clear to me why I thought this. I think I imagined that if I was with him that it would be impossible to work. Subconsciously, I guess, I was simply too overwhelmed by it all and didn't know what to do, and so could do nothing. Couldn't write, couldn't go see this baby.

The third week of January, I rented from this old couple an attic room, which I was going to use as a writing room. A writing room was the solution, I thought. The old couple gave me a wooden chair and I bought a little card table for a desk, and there was already a cot up there in the attic for taking naps. My first day at the card table, I still couldn't write anything for my book. So I wrote this long confessional letter to my teacher at Princeton, Joyce Carol Oates. I told her about my son, my drinking, my hospitalization, and my writing block. Essentially, I was begging for her help. It was a humiliating letter, but I didn't know what else to do. I swooned away from my card table and I took a nap on the cot. When I woke up, I read the letter. How can I mail this? I wondered. How can I burden her with my troubles? But I didn't know who else to turn to.

I put the letter in an envelope and addressed it. Then I opened this little Hazelden meditation book that a friend had given me while I was in the hospital. For each day of the year there was an aphoristic quote from a famous person and then a little paragraph that expanded upon the theme of the quote. I opened the book to the day, to January 23, and the aphorism from the famous person read: "No person can save another." It was attributed to Joyce Carol Oates.

I slid back violently from my desk as if a ghost had yanked my chair out. I hadn't even mailed my letter, but I had received my response. I hid the letter in a book. It was never sent.

From January 23 on I began to write every day. My life settled into a very good routine. I read the diet book *Fit for Life,* not because I needed to lose weight, but because my sister had recommended its methods as a way for me to deal with my difficult (constipated) digestion. Following the book's regimen, I became quite regular every morning—and if I was behind schedule in the A.M., I would wait until the toilet beckoned. I couldn't write in the morning until I had first released my bowels. Usually I was in the attic by nine. I'd work until noon and then repair to my vegetarian restaurant, the Tempting Tiger. Every day I ordered a hummus salad that cost $2.50. Sometimes I splurged and had avocados added for seventy-five cents. My money was tight back then, as it has been for the last ten years. It's so fatiguing to be broke all the time. I'd like to lie down right now thinking about it.

Anyway, after lunch at the Tiger, I would take a brief nap in the attic and then write until five. I would then go to the university gym, where I still had privileges, and play basketball for two hours. Then it was home and a sober salad. *Fit for Life* had taught me that if I wanted to be alive, I had to eat food that was alive.

Then I'd write letters and read until ten. I followed this schedule for months. I had no social life and I had once again sworn off sex. I was frightened of it. I had come to see fornication as my downfall. I had misused the gift of sex and had created an illegitimate child. But I was working hard on my book, working like a monk, so that I could go see this child, my son.

One day in March, though, I went to the supermarket in the middle of the day and this thirty-something graduate student picked me up. We went back to her apartment and she gave me a blowjob. As soon as it was done, I was so racked with guilt that I went running to the enormous, cathedral-like university chapel. I was all alone in there and I prayed to God for forgiveness. But I became so distraught that I lay down on the cold, stone floor of the chapel and hid under the wooden pews. I started writhing there on the floor; it was sort of a strange spasming, swimming motion. Then I thought I felt God opening up my back like an envelope, and this fierce, burning red light was entering me to purify me and to remove my sins. I lay on that floor for at least an hour. I knew I was losing my mind, but I couldn't stop myself.

I wondered as I lay there if I was becoming like the other madmen in town. There were several strange fellows in Princeton who lingered around the campus, like sick birds who can't fly. No one knew their exact histories, but they appeared to be graduate students whose minds had been broken by academia.

There were two such men whom I was particularly fascinated by. One was this tiny, well-dressed fellow with a perfectly circular bald spot on the back of his head. He was forever approaching girls and asking them, "Do you go to Rutgers?" Why he was asking Princeton University coeds if they went to Rutgers was a great mystery. And if they gave him any kind of response, he would then ask them out for dinner. It was harmless enough, but he did this at least a dozen times each day.

He also had the peculiar habit of walking all around Princeton early in the morning while drinking from a pint of milk. Often, because I had insomnia, I would see him out my window at six A.M., tilting back his pint carton. As the months went by, his bald spot seemed to grow larger, and the heels of his shoes were worn down ferociously by his constant walking.

The other broken graduate student who had caught my eye was this man who spent his days in the main library. He was always in this small study room, jokingly called the Hunting and Killing Room because there were watercolors of hunting scenes. He was tall with a yellowish, egglike bald head, and he had this grotesque wreath of stringy black hair that hung from about the level of his ears down to his neck. He looked like a classic pervert, and when I was an undergraduate, the girls called him the Onanist because he would sit in the Hunting and Killing Room and look at the girls and rub himself, but somehow discreetly enough that he was never arrested.

(Years later, because of this man, when I had to come up with a name for my *New York Press* column, I suggested to the editors "The Onanist." And they were very pleased with this, but then I chickened out and asked for it to be called the more elegant "The Boulevardier." But they thought this was too pansy, and they went with my third suggestion, "City Slicker.")

So after my incident on the chapel floor, I thought I might be destined to become a campus ghoul, but somehow I rallied and I kept working on my book all through the spring. I had only one other sexual incident, and that was with the tree outside my attic window. When it flowered in May, it gave off the most erotic odor. I would get unsolicited erections just sitting there at my card table. I fell in love with that tree.

By the end of July 1988, eight months past my deadline, I finished my novel. I wrote by hand back then and first had to deliver the manuscript to a typist, a woman. When she finished, I then mailed the book to my editor and immediately bought a cheap train ticket to Georgia because I couldn't afford to fly. I was finally going to see my son, who was now over two years old.

The night before I was to leave for Georgia, I was on the phone with a friend and there was an emergency break-through by the operator. A doctor from Los Angeles was calling to tell me that both my parents were in critical condition after a terrible car accident— they had been hit head-on at sixty miles per hour by an out-of-control driver who jumped across to their side of the highway. They were in L.A. visiting my sister, who had just moved out there. My sister had also been in the car, but she wasn't in critical condition, though she had serious injuries. My whole family was nearly wiped out, and the doctor told me that my mother was the worst off, that her liver had been crushed, that he wasn't sure whether she would survive.

I called my son's mother, told her what was going on, that my visit would have to be delayed; she was, of course, understanding and kind. Then I went immediately to the airport and got the next flight to California; the airline gave me some kind of emergency ticket. And as I sat on that plane I kept feeling as if the right side of my body was caving in. I didn't consciously know it, but that's where the liver is, and I kept holding myself there; it was like I was a chest of drawers, and the drawer there on my side had been pulled out.

I arrived in L.A. and went first to my mother's hospital. (My parents had been taken to different emergency rooms so that there would be enough surgeons to try and save their lives.) I met her doctor before seeing her. "How is she?" I asked.

"She has a fifty-fifty chance," he said.

I went into her room and her eyes were closed. She was surrounded by the necessary tubes, machines, and pumps. She was only fifty-one, but she looked like she was eighty. Her face had aged—it was white and shrunk and withered. She opened her blue eyes and she saw me and she smiled so radiantly, even through her pain. "Jonathan," she said. "I love you," she said. I put my face next to hers, careful not to hurt her, not to undo anything. "I love you," I said. She held me, and she told me, in a whisper, that a prayer she had learned when I was in the hospital nine months before for drinking had saved her. It saved her while she was being cut out of the car, while the clothes were taken off her body on the side of the road while people stared, while all vanity was lost, while her body felt, as she later wrote in a poem, like "venetian blinds crumbling," while she experienced the most grotesque pain of her life everywhere in her body. So she said this prayer over and over—

thousands of times she thought she had said it; it was her only solace, the prayer she had learned to say to cope with the fact that her son seemed bent on killing himself with alcohol. It went like this: "God grant me the serenity to accept the things I cannot change, the courage to change the things I can, and the wisdom to know the difference."

My mother survived and both my parents were eventually transferred, after a week, to the same hospital, Cedars-Sinai, where they spent three weeks. After Cedars, my sister and I had them moved to a nursing home in Santa Monica, where they spent another three weeks. It took about half a year, but they both made remarkable recoveries from a slew of devastating injuries. My mother lost her spleen, and her liver had been squashed, but was repaired with surgery—the doctor said that God had acted through his hands. All my father's ribs had been broken, his lungs had collapsed, and he had nearly died from misdiagnosed internal bleeding. For the first three days at Cedars, they were unable to see each other because they were on different floors and neither of them was strong enough to get out of bed and into a wheelchair. At the time of the accident, they'd been married thirty-two years, and those ten days apart, first in their different hospitals and then at Cedars, was the longest they had ever been separated from each other. Then on the eleventh day, my father was stronger, and with his I.V. bottle I wheeled him over to my mother, and when she saw him, she said gleefully, "My hero!"

So while they were recuperating those first six weeks, I stayed in L.A. on the floor of my sister's apartment. Then when my parents were well enough to fly, I moved back home with them to drive them to doctors, to cook their meals, to clean the house. My editor sent back my manuscript during this time for some small changes and I finished those quickly. The book was done.

By the end of October of 1988, I was able to leave my parents for a weekend—they could take care of themselves—and I flew down to Georgia.

I was just going to see my son; I wasn't sure what I was going to do, what role I would play in his life. He was two and a half years old now, and all he knew was that a friend of Mommy's was coming to stay for a few days; he didn't know that I was his father. I arrived there late at night, but he woke up and crawled to the end of his bed and peered out his door at me. He was beautiful. Bright red hair, porcelain-white skin. And the most amazing smile came onto his face when he saw me. I approached him and he immediately wanted to climb into my arms, although I was a complete stranger. So I held him and it was perfect. I've been his father ever since.

My Great-Aunt Pearl

IT WAS AROUND NOON and my fiber supplement, ingested at nine, was doing its job and I was sitting on the toilet. Next to my toilet is a mirror. I looked in the mirror and I noticed how tight the skin was on my forehead. I could really see the outline of my cranium and then I imagined my skull without its skin. I saw some Hamlet-like person picking it up out of a grave. Oh, God, I'm going to die someday, I thought. My body, my life will have no significance. I'll be an empty skull.

It was all too depressing, and I flushed and got the hell off that toilet before it sucked me down to my grave. It's so rare for me to actually be pierced by my mortality. I'm too busy being nervous and afraid about being alive to worry about dying.

I sat at my kitchen table, and to keep my life force going, I ate a banana; in these lean financial times I survive on bananas, oatmeal, peanut butter, carrots, and apples. I never thought of it before, but I practically have the diet of a horse. Halfway through the banana the phone rang. It was a woman and she asked, "Are you Jonathan Ames, Pearl's nephew?"

"Yes," I said, concerned. She was talking about my eighty-four-year-old great-aunt who lives in Queens.

"I'm with Meals-on-Wheels and Pearl didn't come to the door today and she didn't call to cancel. And she isn't answering her phone. I've tried reaching her for an hour. You're on our list to call in case of an emergency."

This was terrible. My great-aunt always cancels her meals-on-wheels if she's going to be out. "Should I call the police?" I asked.

"Don't panic. . . . I'm just supposed to call you. Maybe try calling her for a little while. Let me know what you find out."

I'm the relative who lives closest to my great-aunt, so I keep an eye on her. She never had any children of her own and she saw my mother as her daughter, and me and my sister as her grandchildren. She is very dear to me.

So first I called my great-aunt, but there was no answer, and she doesn't have an answering machine. Then I called her neighbor Phyllis, but she wasn't in. Then I called my great-aunt's doctor—perhaps she had an appointment. The receptionist said she did have an appointment but that she had canceled that morning. This frightened me. For my great-aunt to cancel a doctor's appointment would mean that she was actually sick and couldn't get out of her apartment, because she lives for her doctor's appointments—it's her social life, her amusement. It's where she gets attention, attention from men. She's especially in love with her primary caregiver, Doctor Schwartz. And it was her appointment with Schwartz that she had canceled. I envisioned her passed out on her floor. Of late she had been complaining of pain on the left side of her head. I tried calling her again, but no answer. So there was only one thing to do: 911. I gave the operator all the information and said that I'd meet the police at my great-aunt's apartment.

"Am I doing the right thing?" I then asked the emergency operator, a woman with a hard-boiled phone demeanor.

"Oh, yeah," she said. "We get calls like this all the time."

I rushed out of the house and got a cab to Queens. I had about thirty dollars on me, just enough money to get out there. I looked out the taxi window and I was scared. Had my morbid thoughts before the phone call been an omen?

For the six years that I've been living in New York, I've gone to see my great-aunt at least once or twice a month. She cooks me a meal and then we play cards—Hollywood gin is our game.

When I was drinking again in the early nineties, I often went to see her on Sundays with terrible hangovers. One Sunday morning, after having debauched myself the previous night, I was standing on the platform waiting for the R train and I was in bad shape and I had a thirty- to forty-minute subway ride to look forward to. I wanted only one thing to soothe myself: a *New York Times* sports section to read. I said to God that if he gave me a sports section, I would believe in him and stop drinking. At that moment, an older gray-haired man joined me on the platform. He had a fat, Sunday *Times* under his arm. He didn't look like a sports fan, too effete— his shoes had tassels.

"Can I have your sports section?" I asked.

"Why should I give it to you?" he said bitterly. Maybe he could smell the booze on my breath, and I thought, So much for God. Then at that precise moment the N train, not my train, went charging by. It slowed to a stop and the subway door opened in front of me. On the seat across the way was a thin section of the *Times*. It looked like the sports section. I ran like a wild man into the car. I rasped at the girl sitting next to the paper, "Is that yours?" She shook her head no, in a frightened way. It *was* the sports section! I grabbed the thing, spun around, and did a fencing leap off the train just as the door was closing. God had answered me! I couldn't believe it. I immediately wanted to bear witness, but I was alone on the platform—there was no one to tell. The older man with the tassels had taken the N. I held my precious bit of newsprint in my hands. It was incredible. Of all the sections of the paper to be left behind, and of all the subway cars in the long train that the paper should be on the one that stopped right in front of me. . . . Was it God? Would I really have to quit drinking? It was only a sports section.

When I got to Queens, I told my great-aunt, with great excitement, what happened. She was unimpressed *and* she was annoyed with me. "You could have been hurt jumping off like that," she said. "You should have stayed on the N to Queens Plaza and switched."

Over the years, there have been several memorable misadventures with my great-aunt. For my graduation from college, she waxed her legs (in her day she had been very beautiful and vain and had several divorces; she was a tiny, gorgeous redhead), but somehow she overdid the waxing. She burned the inside of her thighs and genitals and had to be in a wheelchair during my commencement. She told all my friends that she had singed her privates.

And then a year later, on our way up to Boston for my sister's graduation from medical school, we stopped at some restaurant on the highway, and my great-aunt ordered a foot-long hot dog. I counseled her against this: "It's bad for your digestion, and it's filled with bone marrow."

"Don't be crazy," she said, and she ate the whole thing. I was horrified, and sure enough, she became stupendously constipated and was miserable in Boston. "It's that hot dog," I kept saying.

"Leave me alone," she'd say. "You're *meshuga.*" But she could hardly enjoy the graduation ceremonies. She was complaining the whole time about being bloated. Finally we took her to a drugstore and she bought herself suppositories. But she didn't look at the package closely, and when we got back to the hotel room, she realized she had bought *infant* suppositories. They were the size of small pencil erasers. But she was very adaptive and she put all twelve of them at once up her *tuches.* Unfortunately, it wasn't enough to dynamite out the hot dog, and she was bad company all the way back to New York.

So as I sat in the cab, I had terrible visions of what I might find in Queens. I wasn't ready to lose her, and I was feeling guilty because I hadn't been out to visit for several weeks.

I was dropped off in front of her building, and I didn't see any police cars. I buzzed her buzzer and the door was clicked open. I took the elevator to the sixth floor, and when I got off, she was there, standing in the hallway. Beautiful and tiny. Her red hair now a whitish orange.

"What's going on?" she said, her voice high-pitched and nervous. "The police were here. Such excitement."

"Meals-on-Wheels called me. They tried to drop off your lunch. They made me think something had happened to you. . . . Where were you?"

"The chiropodist. I had my toenails clipped."

"Well, thank God, you're all right," I said, and I hugged her to my chest.

Then we walked into her small, overheated apartment. "I'm not a shut-in, you know," she said, scolding me. Her pride was wounded;

she didn't want me doubting her independence. "If I don't answer the phone, don't call the police."

"It's Meals-on-Wheels's fault. They called me, alarmed me."

"They're always fouling up," she said. "I called and canceled this morning. Now I'm all shook up."

We sat down in her kitchen. "I'm sorry, Aunt Pearl. I was scared. I didn't know what else to do."

She took off her shoe. "I forgot to have the chiropodist bandage my toe. It's killing me." She had me get a Band-Aid from the drawer, then she put her tiny, misshapen foot on my thigh. From years of wearing high heels, she has bunions the size of elbow joints. She instructed me to part the little toe from the rest and then to wrap the Band-Aid around the nail. Her toes were yellow, from the chiropodist's iodine, I think, and the little nails were embedded and ancient, but I was glad to hold her foot and bandage her toe. Then I rubbed her sole and she smiled at me. Then we had lunch and played gin. It turned out to be a good visit.

A Christmas Eve Sojourn

THE FIRST COUPLE OF YEARS of my son's life, I was often low on money and so I was always looking for the cheapest way to get to Georgia, and this particular Christmas of 1989, I was getting there by train and bus.

I was living in Princeton at the time and I made the first leg of the journey with my new girlfriend. We took an overnighter on Amtrak from Newark to Charleston, South Carolina, which was where her family had recently moved. I had one little backpack with me and this big cardboard box that I had fashioned together with rope and a special handle; in the box were all my son's toys.

My girlfriend and I had only been together a few weeks and we were in that early stage of making love all the time. We tried to do it in the train bathroom, but people kept jiggling the handle and this threw off my performance.

When we arrived in Charleston on the twenty-third of December, we were met by her big Catholic family. Both her parents, I knew, were a little suspicious of me—I was Jewish and an older man. My girlfriend was twenty-one and I was twenty-five, and this difference of four years was considered significant. But despite these suspicious qualities—my Jewishness and my age—her parents were also welcoming. Her mother kissed me on the cheek and her father crushed my hand—he was an ex–army man, an officer in the Vietnam War, and only recently retired. But despite her parents' initial warmth and hospitality, my girlfriend and I thought it was too soon to inform them that I had a son, so we told them that I'd be going on to Georgia the next day to be with cousins.

That night after a lovely pre–Christmas Eve dinner, her father lent us the family van so that we could go for a ride. We drove around for a little while—my girlfriend didn't know the area since her parents had just moved there—and then on our way back, near her house, we found a semideserted dead end where we thought we could do a little old-fashioned parking. There was one street lamp and a few houses set back from the road. We started to make love—it had been nearly forty-eight hours, a long stretch for us at that time—and the van was rocking happily. The backseat was tilted down and we were on top of it and I was on top of her. It was a little awkward—she was a tall and leggy blonde—but we managed; I was more athletic in those days.

At some point in my efforts, I noticed that the shadow of her head in the back window seemed to be moving from side to side. How unusual, I thought, since we were loving one another in a north-south direction. I ignored this phenomena, but then I looked up again and it struck me as too curious that her head wasn't aligning with its shadow. So without saying anything, trying to make it seem like an interesting gesture of affection, I moved her head a little to the left. But the shadow, now still, didn't move accordingly.

My girlfriend's eyes were closed and she was happily moaning. She was unaware that I was conducting an experiment, an experiment that I intuitively sensed was tinged with doom, and I moved her head to the right. Again the shadow didn't move. Then it hit me—the doom revealed itself—the shadow was being cast by someone else's head from the outside. Her father, the veteran! I screamed and made a hasty, wild coital retreat. She screamed. I pulled my pants up, which were at my ankles, quicker than I had ever done anything in my life.

"There's someone out there!" I bellowed. "No!" she cried abstractly, and covered her breasts with her hands. Her father had found us and was going to shoot me with his old service revolver.

The car was lit with a flashlight. Of course, a military man would have a powerful flashlight. But then I saw an angry, contorted face pressed again the rear window. It was a scowling black man. "Get the fuck out of here! Fucking on my street!" he shouted, and then he slammed his hand on the roof of the car.

My poor girlfriend was shrieking. I got into the driver's seat and I fumbled like a movie-ass with the keys—life is at its most horrible when you find yourself re-creating stock Hollywood scenes. Then I gathered some coordination, ignited the car, and pulled out of there.

Our getaway successful, we pulled over a few minutes later and we calmed each other; we even laughed a little. Then back at her parents' house, we had tea and freshly baked Christmas cookies with her mother in the kitchen. Her father was already asleep, since he still woke each day at five A.M.

As I sat there eating cookies, my groin felt strange, oddly absent, so I excused myself and went to the bathroom for an inspection. My penis was utterly inverted and numb. The sudden withdrawal had done something to me. I was in some kind of genital shock.

Later, when we were alone, I said to my girlfriend, though I was afraid to be saying such things in a Catholic, military home, "I think something has happened to my penis. I may have damaged it."

"Don't be ridiculous," she said.

We went into the bathroom and she took a look at it. "It is very small," she said.

"Please," I said, "don't make things worse."

"Well, I've never seen it this small."

She tried to breathe some life into the thing, but this only frightened me more. My initial reaction that the shadow-head was her father hadn't fully left me; my nervous system was still expecting to be shot. "Please, stop," I said. "Your father is going to come in here and cut it off with a bayonet."

She laughed and I got out of the bathroom in one piece. I spent the night on the couch by the large Christmas tree, and the smell of pine needles was soothing.

Early the next morning, we went to the bus station. I bought a ticket for a small town in Georgia, which was the closest stop to my son's small town, even though it was forty miles away. Before leaving Charleston, I called down to Georgia, where my son lived on a farm with his mother, older sister (not my daughter), and grandmother, to let them know when I'd be arriving. The grandmother and my son would be picking me up; my son's mother and her daughter were going to the coast and would return Christmas afternoon.

It was to be a twelve-hour bus ride, but I had a book and several magazines. And my girlfriend prepared two nice sandwiches that I was to ration out over the course of the journey.

I put the box filled with my son's toys in the belly of the bus, my girlfriend and I had a chaste kiss good-bye—her mother was in the van watching—and then I headed out of South Carolina, glad to be alive, but still concerned with the strange absenteeism in my groin.

The trip was fairly miserable. People in the last few rows could still smoke in buses back then and so I was sucking on the air that came through the edge of the window. Sometimes I lifted my shirt over my mouth and tried to filter the smoke that way. I was sitting near the front and I would turn around and give the smokers withering glances to shame them, but it had no effect.

I ate both my sandwiches by noon and cursed myself for my lack of character. Then I walked to the back of the bus, into the inferno of smoke, and went in the ghastly toilet. I checked myself out and my penis was still in shock. I tried a little onanism, but the cigarette smoke and the toilet smell got to me. I returned to my seat.

Around one o'clock a young, pimply, yellow-haired girl, about sixteen, got on the bus and sat next to me. She wasn't much to look at, but she was wearing a short skirt and I could see Georgia peach fuzz on the top of her thighs.

"Where are you going this Christmas Eve day?" I asked, trying to hide my lechery.

"To see my grandparents," she said.

Then she promptly, almost narcoleptically, fell asleep, and the darling's little head rested on my shoulder. I inhaled the raw teenagey smell of her scalp. This unexpected intimacy caused a rebirth of sensation in my groin. I was happy to be back to normal, but it was mildly uncomfortable to have an erection, which the rocking of the bus kept alive, as did the touch of her head on my shoulder. I tried a yoga breath to draw the air out of my penis, something I learned in a tantric book, but it didn't work.

Luckily, the girl got off the bus two hours later and I was able to relax. But not for long. Toward evening, a torrential rainstorm began and I was afraid that the driver was getting weary. To die in a bus on Christmas Eve seemed a lousy fate. I had a small child waiting for me. I coughed loudly a few times to try and rouse the driver. He needed all his powers of concentration on these wet, dark Southern roads.

Around eight o'clock, it was still raining, and the bus pulled into a tiny station and it was announced that this was the last stop. But it wasn't *my* stop. Something was wrong. The driver directed me to the manager of the station. A terrible mistake had been made. In Charleston, I had been issued the wrong ticket—on holidays the bus didn't continue to my destination, and Christmas Eve was considered a holiday. I was fifty miles away from where I was supposed to be.

I called my son's house, but there was no answer, and no answering machine. My son and his grandmother had obviously left to come meet me.

"What am I going to do?" I asked the station manager—a heavy man with a kind bald head and a company-issued narrow blue tie.

"You'll have to call a taxi. They'll take you to the other station."

I called the one taxi in town—I was deep in Georgia farm country—but there was no answer. The taxi company must have closed for Christmas Eve.

I started to panic. I couldn't think straight; I had been inhaling secondhand smoke for hours on end. Then the lights in the bus station were flickered, like at a Broadway show. The station was closing down.

"What should I do?" I asked the manager.

"Your family will probably figure out what happened and come pick you up here."

Then he had the good idea to call the other station, so that they could find my son's grandmother and explain to her the mistake that had occurred. So he called and there was no answer.

"I guess they're closed for the night," he said. "And I'm sorry, but I got to lock up, too." This was Southern Gothic hell. He then reassured me that my family would figure out where I was, or if they didn't, that when they got home I could call them—there was a phone outside the station—and they would come get me.

I explained to the man that this whole process could take hours: They lived forty miles from the other station, and this would mean driving ninety miles in pouring rain with a three-year-old eager to see his nutty daddy. The station manager said he was sorry about all this, but there was nothing he could do.

Then he locked up the joint and I went and stood under the awning outside. It was a tiny bus station, in a small, Christmas Eve–darkened town. I stood by the phone with the box of my son's toys, waiting like a tragic fool. I was utterly alone. Something out of a Flannery O'Connor story was going to happen to me. A serial killer was going to tell me I'd be a good man if there was a gun to my head my whole life.

I watched the rain smash against the asphalt lot. I tried to count the drips off the awning. I was starving. It had been hours since I had foolishly eaten both sandwiches. God is punishing me, I thought, for trying to make love in the train bathroom, fornicate in the van, and masturbate on the bus. I had been sinning the whole way down to Georgia. I thought of calling the police. Let them throw me in jail for the night. Then there were headlights on me. Good, I thought, the police have responded to me telepathically. The car door opened. It was the bus manager.

"I couldn't let you just wait here in this storm. I'll drive you to the station."

I got in the man's car. He was sacrificing his Christmas Eve dinner for me. It was an act of unexpected, heroic American kindness. I thanked him as graciously as I could, then he bored me for an hour with tales of the bus world—as in all work, he was plagued by internal politics. But I listened with enthusiasm—it was the least I could do. We arrived at the other station, and in the still-pouring rain, they were there, sitting in the car in a darkened lot, waiting for me.

In the car window, my son's face, framed by his yellow raincoat, was so expectant and beautiful. No one in my life has ever been so happy to see me.

I thanked the bus manager heartily and asked for his address. I wrote him a thank-you note the next day, and also sent a letter of praise to his bus company. When I got into the car with my son, I was showered with kisses. "I love you, I love you," he said repeatedly, which is what he used to do when he would first see me back then.

His sweet grandmother drove us to the farm. The rain made the road slick and dangerous, and my son said, "Look, the lights are melting on the street." It was the kind of thing parents and grand-parents love to hear from their children, and indeed the lights did look like they were melting. By the time we got home, he was asleep and I carried him in. I thanked his grandmother for picking me up, and then she retired for the night. I opened the cardboard box and put my son's toys under the tree. I went to sleep and when I woke up it was Christmas.

The Shroud of Onan

S ATURDAY MORNING, the blighted sun came through my window, awakening me. Actually it came through the stained sheet
that I had hung recently over my window to *block out* the sun. It's
a blue sheet from my days in Brooklyn, and the sun illumined all
these islands of brownish discoloration, like liver spots on an elderly
person's hands. Back in Brooklyn I was in such a state of melancholy and slovenliness that I didn't have a designated masturbation
cleanup towel. So my onanistic eructations were absorbed by the
sheet on the side of the bed where I didn't sleep. And no one else
ever slept on that side. Who wants to sleep with other people? It's
hard enough to get a good night's sleep by myself.

So I stared at the islands of stains, surprised actually that there
were large clear areas, and the blue color made it all seem sealike.
That sheet is a map of my former indiscretions and excretions. It
looks like a chain of islands, like Indonesia . . . well, more like
Hawaii because there's one large blot that must have been a favorite
spot for me. I studied this map, alternately amused and depressed
that I should use a semen-stained sheet for a curtain, and then I
roused myself, swung my legs out of my bed, and immediately
stepped on a paper clip, which had just enough of a little point

sticking up so that it was like falling in one of those pits in Vietnam with spears. I gave a healthy scream and thought to myself, I should step on that paper clip more often. It's good for waking me up.

Then the phone rang. It was my father. He was calling from Queens. He had just collected my great-aunt Pearl and now he was coming to get me to take me home to New Jersey for the weekend. Sunday was Mother's Day and I was going home for two days to celebrate my good and dear mother.

I waited outside my building and a strong wind brought to my highly developed nostrils the smell of the sea. All this recent spring wind and rain keeps bringing to my nose hints of salt water, reminding me that New York is surrounded by water, that it is an island—a huge stain of land and man and pizza parlors and massage parlors and banks and coffee places. Not a bad place to live except your soul dies from a lack of contact with nature. There's plenty of human nature, but so much of it that it's deadly.

The smell of the sea in my nose made me want to travel. *Call me collect*—to add more abuse to Melville's famous line—and take me on a trip, somebody, please. I'll pay for the call, you pay for the trip. I'd like to go to Europe. I'd like to have a drinking relapse in Ireland. I'd like to go to Turkey, where I'm held in esteem as a writer— they've already started translating my new novel. My editor from Istanbul called me long distance. He said, "I think in America you get the recognition you don't deserve." Of course, he screwed up the English, but I know the true meaning of what he was trying to say. I do hope, though, he understands my book properly.

My father picked me up; we headed for New Jersey. I yearn for the Continent and I get the Garden State. My great-aunt was in the backseat—tiny and a bit loony, her beautiful orange-red hair shaped in a bowl cut. She was smiling, happy. She was being liberated from Queens, going to *Jersey,* as she always calls it. I reached my hand back to her; she took it and kissed it enthusiastically many times. "I love you, I love you," she said.

I said hello to my father and he grunted. He's often surly and hostile with me at first, and then he warms up. It's our old Oedipal struggle. Ancient, classic anger between father and son. Jealousy and competition. Someday I'll write a column about it; I already have the title: "Oedipissed Off."

We took the FDR. My great-aunt said to me, "What size neck are you?"

"Sixteen," I said. We've gone over this a thousand times.

"Your arms?"

"Thirty-three."

"I'll get you a shirt at NBO . . . Polo. Do you know Polo?"

"Yes."

"Do you want a dark blue or a light blue?"

"Don't buy me any shirts. Don't spend your money."

"Do you want a dark blue or a light blue?"

"Dark."

I always give in. She buys me ugly shirts, but it makes her happy, gives her something to do—a trip to the NBO near Queens Boulevard.

We passed Yankee Stadium. "How's my boyfriend, Davey Cohen, pitching?" she asked.

I tried to tell her once that it was Cone. That he's not Jewish. But she prefers her delusion. Ever since Koufax, the Jews need somebody. "Pretty good," I said about Cone. "He only lasts six innings, but the Yankee bullpen is strong."

We arrived in New Jersey. The rain was coming down. I needed nature, but this nature was too wet. I kissed my mother and hugged her. "I've come home to be with you," I said gallantly. Then I retreated to the basement to radiate myself in front of the television. That's what I always do when I go home. I spend hours microwaving myself—my parents have thousands of channels. I have a TV here in New York, but it only gets Channel 4.

I watched the Knicks win their game against the Pacers. Then we all had a nice late lunch. Then I went back down to the basement and watched *Splash*. I hadn't seen it in years. I wept the entire movie. I hate it when Hollywood does that to me. I've spent so much time crying in the darkness of my parents' basement.

When I wasn't crying during *Splash,* I was admiring Darryl Hannah's ass when she runs into the ocean. Then at one point I wondered, Where *is* Darryl Hannah? She has disappeared, but I'm glad. That means someday Uma Thurman and Gwyneth Paltrow will disappear. My system can hardly tolerate the existence of these blondes. They make the average subaverage male feel like life will always be inadequate because you won't get to bed one of these beauties. You end up bedding your own bedding and hanging it like a flag of your submaleness in your window.

After *Splash,* I went upstairs to take a bath. Whenever I'm home, I watch television or I take really long baths. Before I filled the tub, I showered off so that I could kick at things I thought I saw on the floor of the tub and send them down the drain. It's a neurosis of mine, more Oedipal stuff—I don't want contact with detritus from my father. But once the tub seemed properly cleared of any offending flakes of unknown origin, I then filled the thing up and lolled in there a good forty minutes, meditating. I always practice a watered-down Buddhism in the bathtub. My great-aunt banged on the door at a particularly profound moment. My whole head was submerged except for my nose.

"What are you doing in there? Are you alive?" she cried. Then she called out to my mother. "Maybe he knocked his head on something. He could be drowning."

"I'm all right," I shouted. "Leave me alone. I was on the verge of enlightenment!"

"Do you want to play cards?" asked my great-aunt, unfeeling about my spiritual development.

I got out and we played cards, and then the whole family took a nap. We woke up at eight and had dinner and then my father and I watched *Three Days of the Condor*. What a great movie. I hadn't seen it in years. I didn't remember the great sex scene with Faye Dunaway and Robert Redford. It was very arousing. Dunaway was moaning realistically. I put my hand in my pocket and jiggled myself. And in the darkened silence of the basement, the hostilities between my father and myself seemed to evaporate. We don't always talk that well, but we watch television together quite nicely.

Around midnight we all went back to sleep. I was lying in my childhood bed thinking about Darryl Hannah's ass and Faye Dunaway's mouth, and the old hand snuck down under the covers. But I didn't want to go through with it. I had turned off the lights and I was too lazy to find something to clean myself up with. But the images from the movies were too powerful. I'll just use the sheet, I thought. My mother won't notice one stain when she does the laundry. But then I thought, How selfish of me to do such a thing when I'm home for Mother's Day.

But I was too weak and so I was biting Hannah's ass and kissing Dunaway's mouth and I was on the verge of explosion, but then my great-aunt burst into my room, which she always does without knocking. The light from the hallway put a glow around her. My blanket shielded me, but I yanked up my underwear and my hand flew away from my groin.

"What are you doing in here?" I shouted. "I was just falling asleep!"

"Do you have today's paper? I need to read something."

"It's downstairs. Leave me alone."

She came and kissed me on the forehead, almost putting her hand right on my erection as she steadied herself. Instead, her hand pinned down the blanket around my protuberance, causing a pleasing tightening sensation, and my penis must have misinterpreted this as a caress from Darryl Hannah—I had been right on the verge—and I ejaculated. I did so silently, just a slight physical *and* psychic shudder. Then my great-aunt left, unaware of my release. I had reached an unbelievable new low. A moment of near-incest with my octogenarian great-aunt. There was only one consolation: I had erupted in my underwear and not on my mother's sheet—it was the least I could do on the eve of her day.

Taxi Stand

I USED TO BE A TAXI DRIVER, but not here in New York City, which would be a romantic claim of sorts; rather, I was a cabbie in suburban Princeton, New Jersey. As a taxi driver there, you didn't roam the streets looking for fares, you waited on line at this taxi stand in the center of town. And people would either walk up to your cab or they would call this one phone that all of us drivers shared. The phone was in this gray metal box, and over the phone was a lightbulb that would flash with each call. It was exciting when the light would flash.

And if I was sitting in my cab, first in line, and the bulb would flicker, I'd hop out fast, like a fireman responding to an alert. Some taxi drivers strolled to the phone, feigning indifference, as if they were above it all, but I always ran. What if the caller hung up? And I never knew who would be on the other end of the line. Could be a job to Newark Airport, $65! Or it could be some Princeton matron wanting a lift to the supermarket, $3.50. But that was one of the thrills of taxi driving—the element of chance and luck. Would it be a day of little money or big money? But regardless, and this was the other great thing about taxi driving, you'd have cash in your pocket at the end of your shift—your labors were immediately rewarded; no waiting two weeks for some computerized paycheck that you felt no connection to. I only made about sixty dollars for twelve hours of driving, but I loved having the money in hand—the day had meaning.

I drove a taxi for two years, from 1990 to 1992, and it was something of a humbling experience. In '87, I had graduated from Princeton. In '89, I was living in the town for purposes of writerly solitude and quiet when my first book came out. I became a local celebrity; the town paper ran a front-page story. But by '90, I was broke and couldn't get a job. No one would hire a novelist. They all thought I'd be taking off at some point. And I would have; by this time I wanted to get the hell out of Princeton, the solitude hadn't done me any good—I had written half of a failed second novel called *The Jewish Duke of Windsor.* But I couldn't get out of town. I'm terrible with money and I just didn't have enough cash to stage a move. So I needed work, but I couldn't even get a clerking job in the library. Only the taxi owners would take me on.

The taxi stand was right by the gates of the university, and I'd sit on this one bench with my fellow drivers. They were a ragged crew of recent immigrants from the West Indies and Haiti—the new guard—along with a bunch of ancient white and black men—the old guard. The drivers who had been around for a while, to my eyes, looked like their cabs. There was Campbell, an elegant Southern black man who had worked in the post office most of his life but for the last fifteen years had driven a taxi. He always wore clean, pressed pants and a nice shirt and beautiful hats. The hats almost never came off, such that when they did, it was a revelation to see his brown, bald head. He liked to sit in his car and smoke cigars and read newspapers while waiting on line. When the phone light went on, and it was his turn, he took his time answering the call. He preferred to read his paper. His cab was a powder-blue Ford with a white top, and the body was shiny and on the front seat he kept a beautiful old cigar box filled with hard candies and coins and pictures of his grandchildren. Everything about him was elegant and smart. He told me that if he had been born in a different time, he might have ended up being a doctor, or at least a pharmacist, but as a black man born in the twenties, he went right into the army during the war and from there went to work for the post office. So Campbell looked like his cab—shiny and old-fashioned, with character inside and the white roof like his hats.

Smiley was an older Italian man, in his mid-sixties or so, who had been driving in Princeton for more than thirty years, but he knew he would never set the Princeton record—which is also the *world* record—for taxi-driving longevity, which was achieved by this man called Irish. All the drivers had nicknames or went by one name, usually their last, and Irish (his nickname) drove for sixty years, from the twenties to the eighties—from *his* twenties to *his* eighties. So Smiley had put in long years, but he never would beat Irish, which he often acknowledged. (On the nickname front: One driver was called London because he had been a taxi driver in London and had learned from the *book* there. In London, there's some kind of taxi-driving book you have to study, and London in Princeton, who was born in Spain, was proud of his knowledge, and if he got into an argument with some other taxi driver, he would dismiss him by saying, "You don't know anything. I know the *book.*" So everybody called him London. And sometimes Jack London because his first name was actually Jack. For a little while I worked for London, drove his car while he was suspended by the police for supposedly pulling a knife on a Princeton student, but then he got his license back and I was employed by this very nice West Indian man named Henry, who worked for the university in Building Services and on the side had a fleet of two cabs.)

So Smiley was distinctive for two things: He chain-smoked Parliaments and had a lifelong limp from polio. One leg was shorter than the other and he was always shaking out the bad one, the short one, like he was trying to get something to slide out of his pocket and down his leg. Nobody made fun of him for that leg-jiggling, but they called him Smiley because no matter what, and he was pretty cantankerous, his face was creased permanently into a smile, maybe from all the smoking. And his car was a simple dull blue, just like the windbreaker he always wore, and his back tires were raised up—he liked them that way—and it seemed like the right one was higher, kind of off the way his body was.

Then there was Jimmy, this ex-cop, and he never spoke to anyone—he was trying to hold on to his cop pride. He drove a station wagon that had a square rear, which looked like Jimmy's big square rear in his khaki pants.

And so it went, everybody looked like their cab, and I wondered over time if I was starting to look like mine—a big, dusty brown ten-year-old Chevy Caprice. Something was wrong with the fuel line and I had to really put my foot down on the pedal to get it to move, so I often thought to myself that for twelve hours I was pushing that heavy car, and I wondered if like the car I was just becoming old and dirty and dying. Mostly I thought that at the end of the day, but by morning, by six A.M. when I'd be back out there, with some coffee in me, I'd be hopeful all over again for a good day, a trip to the airport if I was lucky.

So every day I'd be sitting on the bench by the taxi stand, usually drinking yet another coffee and complaining with my cohorts about the slowness of business, and my former professors would go strolling past me. At first they said hello, but then because it was embarrassing for me and them—I was on that bench for two years, after all; it looked like I was becoming a taxi lifer—they would simply ignore me, which was the most reasonable thing to do.

Since Princeton is trapped in some kind of *Winesburg, Ohio* time warp, it is the ideal setting for an old-fashioned American short story—the town is populated with gin-drinking alcoholics, horny, neglected housewives, gimps, crazed professors, lunatic children of professors, and rich snobs with secret weaknesses. So one day the town gimp, Charlie, ambled up to my cab. Charlie was in his forties and had been hit by a truck as a child. He dragged his right leg around and his right arm was spastic. He was thin and wiry and had a thick brown beard. His voice was oddly high-pitched. He spent his days sweeping (with his good arm) the sidewalks in front of stores. He demanded money for this task and the merchants took pity on him, even though Charlie's personality was grating. He was mildly retarded (either from the truck or before) but in an annoying way—he harangued people. He was always after me to give him free rides, which I sometimes did. And he'd fill my whole cab with a terrible sweaty smell, like a salty mudflat, and I'd drive him to the outskirts of town, where he lived in a small subsidized apartment. But on this one day in September of '90, early in the morning, he got into my backseat and said, "Take me to Atlantic City. I'm on a roll!"

I turned and looked at him with annoyance. With his good hand he yanked out of his pocket a thick wad of bills. "I'll give you one-fifty," he said. It was a deal. Of that one-fifty, I'd make seventy-five—everything was split with the boss. I could make the round-trip in three hours. I'd have a day's pay before noon.

It was a beautiful ride to Trumpville—we took the old two-lane highways through the endless trees of the Pine Barrens. The sun was perfect, the sky was a clean, infinite blue. Charlie smelled, but I was willing to tolerate it for the money. He was quiet back there, but every time we passed a sign announcing the miles to Atlantic City, he'd gleefully shout out, "Sixty-eight miles to go! . . . Forty-seven miles to go!" and so on. Between these outbursts, I did procure from him an explanation for this voyage. At the end of every month he got his check from the government and so he'd take a bus to the casinos and play blackjack. He usually lost most of the money, but this time he had won big and he wanted to get back there right away to keep his roll going. Over the next two years, Charlie had a few good rolls and I was always his personal driver to A.C. Sometimes I'd stop and play a few hands myself, but that first time I watched him limp into Caesar's and then I turned right around. I wanted to have a big day on the taxi stand.

But on my way back that first time through the Pine Barrens— New Jersey's equivalent of *Deliverance* country—I stopped at a small, white, aluminum-sided porno shack. Why I had to do this, I don't know. It must be my constant need to sully the sacred with the profane. Amidst all these beautiful endless miles of pine trees (the Barrens is one of the largest virgin forests in America), I was compelled to look at the garish boxes of porn videos. The store was tiny and had a limited selection, and there were no magazines. A rugged, Hell's Angel type was the *padrone* behind the cash register. I was about to leave, but then I noticed that there was a door in the far corner. Above it was a sign that read, MISTRESS SUPERIOR, DOMINANCE SESSIONS. A dominatrix in the Pine Barrens? Like a child in a C. S. Lewis story reaching slowly for what should not be reached, I walked over and knocked at the door. It opened immediately. A woman in her late forties, all got up in black bra, garters, heels, eerie blood-red lipstick, spooky blue eyeshadow, and with dyed yellow hair, stood before me. Her large breasts were covered with frightening dark-brown sunspots.

"You want a session?"

"Yes."

She took my arm and pulled me in. She closed the door. I was in a large crimson closet. It was lit by red bulbs. At the end of the closet was a cushioned bench. Above my head was a shelf that went along all the walls, and it was lined with hundreds of oddly shaped candles. Wait, not candles, butt plugs! An incredible collection, so diverse. And hanging on the walls below the shelves were whips and riding crops and handcuffs.

"Eighty-five for the hour," she said. Her breath smelled of cigarettes. We were in close quarters. Eighty-five was too much money; it would negate the whole trip to A.C.

"I'm sorry, but I can't afford you," I said.

"How much can you afford?"

I had to get out of there. I was going to get cancer from the proximity to the sun blemishes on her breasts and from the cigarette breath. I stated a price that I thought would have her kick me out. Fifteen dollars.

"All right," she said. "I'll give you ten minutes for that."

Next thing I knew I was giving her the fifteen bucks. Even my green money looked red in that closet.

"What do you like to do?" she asked.

"I don't know," I said.

So she took over. She had me put my hands against the wall above the bench. "Spread 'em," she said, referring to my legs. I did. Then the pants were down. Then a foreign object was up my ass. One of the butt plugs!

"Did you wash that thing?" I asked meekly over my shoulder.

"Shut up," she said, but then she added, "I'm very clean. I scald my plugs and soak 'em in rubbing alcohol."

Then she reached her arm around my neck, choked me for a second, and then slapped me. After the slap, she lowered her arm and began a coarse, pumping handjob. Her cancerous tits were on my back. Her cigarette breath was warm on my neck. She whispered, "You're a little shit." She pumped. "Mama's boy," she said, and that struck a nerve—it was true, or something. I came on the floor. She yanked out the butt plug. Handed me a paper towel to clean up my mess. My poor wasted sperm—little glowing red droplets on the floor, my life force. She handed me a garbage can for the towel.

Then I was out of there, in my taxi, driving back to Princeton. To the town and the gown. I thought of Mistress Superior whispering, "Mama's boy." I got a post-perverted-sex hard-on. I took stock. The day wasn't entirely lost. I was still ahead sixty dollars.

III
Difficulties

Father Smells Best

MY SON CAME UP FOR his summer visit. He's a big kid now. Twelve years old. Hair under the armpits. Pimples on the chin. He's five-foot-seven, one hundred forty pounds. I have only five pounds on my little Oedipal challenger. He's not fat, just incredibly solid. One of his ankles is as thick as both of mine. He's going to be well over six feet. In the ring, I'll have to rely on quickness and parental authority to take him out.

He looks just like me, has my features: bent nose, albino eyebrows, no lips, blue eyes. His hair is a dark red. My hair used to be that color, but as I've gotten older, it's fallen out and the red has turned yellow like my eyes (my eyes are yellow because of my relatively benign liver condition—Gilbert's Syndrome).

My son's not a precocious New York City kid; he lives on his farm in Georgia. He spent a couple of years in a trailer. I'd visit him in the trailer. Trailers aren't bad. More room in them than you'd think because things are miniaturized—the shower, the kitchen table. It's like being in an airplane toilet. You appreciate the efficiency of the design; you feel like a giant.

So he's not one of these Manhattan youngsters with a depraved, sophisticated vocabulary, but somewhere he picked up the word *dop-*

pelgänger. From a comic book, I think. He says to me, "I'm your doppelgänger." We look like a big brother and a little brother, and because I'm immature, that's more the style of our relationship, though he calls me Dad. And this, when I reflect a moment, is sometimes still strange for me. I didn't meet my son until he was over two years old, and ten years later, it can still feel like a shock, a revelation—I'm someone's father. I see him about every two months. It's a schizophrenic lifestyle. With his arrival, I go from perverted bachelorhood to responsible single parenthood in an instant.

This visit he was with me for three weeks. We started out in New Jersey at my parents' house. That's where I usually spend time with him. Sometimes we camp out in my apartment in New York—I have a futon for him—but this time we stayed out of the hot city. So we fished on the lake where I grew up. Last summer I caught a five-pound bass; this summer they weren't biting as well. Still, we caught a few. Naturally, I got a hook stuck in the gullet of one fish and had to cut the line. I'm lousy at getting hooks out. That poor beautiful fish probably died, though my son and I always hold on to the fishermen's myth that the hook rusts out. But you never know if this is true. I wonder if my bad karma with the fish will affect the sales of my book; it comes out very soon.

After a couple of days in Jersey, my parents, my son, and I all went to L.A. to see my sister and her three-month-old twins, a boy and a girl. My résumé is growing: son, brother, father, uncle. It was my first time seeing the babies, and I held my little niece and nephew, one at a time, against my chest. Sometimes they farted and I would gush for my son's pleasure: "It's an Ames!" We do a lot of our bonding around fart jokes.

I loved holding the little babies. And *they* held on to me, their miniature hands grabbing hold of my manly chest hairs. They are extremely tiny—premature like most twins—and I was able to support their little diapered buttocks with the palm of my hand, and with my other hand I cradled their heads, since their necks are too weak to provide support. I never held my son as a newborn, though I did get a chance to change his diapers. He'd cry a lot, lying there nude and soiled, so I'd put the fresh diaper on my head, and this always amused him.

When I was holding my sister's babies, I worried about the soft spot on the top of their heads. I've never liked hearing about that soft spot. I wish such things didn't exist. You touch that soft spot in the wrong way and the child is retarded for life. You have to wait years for that soft spot to harden. I find it nerve-racking. Children should wear bicycle helmets twenty-four hours a day. So I was very gentle with these precious twins, and my father saw how careful I was being and he said, "You know, babies can withstand a lot. You fell off a dresser and you're relatively normal."

"What happened to my dad?" asked my son, excitedly. He always loves tales of my injuries and defeats and humiliations. Takes great pleasure in them. I can't tell you how many times he's asked me to retell the story of how I shit in my pants in the South of France after eating a poisonous tuna-fish sandwich.

"Well, we left him with a baby-sitter one night," said my dad, regaling my son. "And when we came home, the poor girl was crying, hysterical. She had put your father on a dresser to change him. Then she turned around for a second to get a diaper and he fell off. On his head. A good four feet. To linoleum. We took him to the doctor the next day, but the doctor said he was fine. So then I was more concerned with the baby-sitter; she was having a nervous breakdown until we told her that your father was all right. But that fall could explain a lot of things."

My father laughed and so did my son. I hadn't heard this story for years and had managed to forget about it, to repress it. But now

I envisioned myself falling off a dresser. It was an unpleasant image, especially since my sister's babies had sensitized me as to the fragility of infants. "This is upsetting," I said. "I can't believe I was dropped on my head. I'm lucky I didn't land on my soft spot."

"Who said you didn't?" said my father.

"Tell me again what happened," said my son. He has started puberty, but like a small child, he still has a great appetite for repetition.

For some reason I was good at holding my niece and nephew—the little kids would stop crying and pass out as soon as they got into my arms. My sister, the doctor, conjectured that because of our similar genetic makeup, I must smell like her, and so the babies found my odor familiar and comforting.

My son thought this was ridiculous. He said that the kids were passing out because of the toxic nature of my odor. He thinks I smell awful because I don't use deodorant. And this is all very sad, because when he was a little kid, he loved my smell. When I'd pick him up at the airport, he'd hold my hand and his head would be level with my wrist and he'd always press his nose against my forearm. "You always smell the same," he'd say happily, visit after visit. It was his way to get to know me again in some primal, essential manner. The smell must have meant that he was with his crazy dad again. Like me, he lives through his nose. Then about a year ago, he said to me, "I figured out what that smell is—B.O.! All these years I've been smelling B.O.!" He saw this as cruelly, though comically, ironic since his sensibilities have been formed by exposure to the Simpsons, Beavis and Butthead, *Mad* magazine, and my own worldview. So all this to say that my little son, who once sniffed my arm like a lover, is growing up.

We had one moment of tension in L.A., my son and I. We were playing Marco Polo in the pool with my sister's nine-year-old step-daughter, Andrea. I questioned my son's bravery in the game and unwittingly embarrassed him in front of the little girl. He then quit the game and Andrea and I continued playing. This deepened his injury and he went inside. When he reemerged some time later, I asked, "What's going on? Why'd you disappear?"

He wouldn't tell me. His face was near-trembling, he was almost crying. Somehow a game of Marco Polo had become a psycholog-ical piece of dynamite. I asked him again what was the matter.

"I don't know you well enough to tell you," he said, fighting tears. I took a breath. This was important, crucial. He was trying to hurt me, but he also needed me. His deep resentment and pain at our not being together all the time, usually unvoiced, was coming out.

"I can appreciate that," I said. "Though I do think you know me pretty well, but what can I do to help you know me better?"

No answer. "There must be something I can do."

"Send me one of your columns," he said. This was unexpected. Then I remembered I had failed in my promise months and months ago to send him the shitting in the South of France column. And the columns in general must be a symbol of my life apart from him, a life that other people know about, but not him.

"I'll send you a column. Is there anything else I can do?"

He was quiet, far away. "Listen," I said. "I know I'm a part-time dad, but I love you very much and I'm very proud of you."

"Why are you proud of me?" The kid was giving me a good working over. Testing me. I was frightened that I would screw up, but glad that he was talking to me.

"Well," I said, "I like the way you think about things, talk about things . . . what a good guest you are here at your aunt's. I'm proud of how you know everything about bicycles. I like your sense of humor. You're fun to travel with. I'm proud of how well you did in school this year. And I'm proud of how big you are, how good-looking and strong. I'm just proud of *you*."

He looked me in the eye. "Thank you," he said. Then we went inside and watched a video with Andrea. Midway through the video he and Andrea launched a tickle attack on me. Everything was all right again.

Oedipus Erects

IN THE SPRING OF 1991, I escaped from Princeton and the taxi stand for a few weeks and went up to this famous artists' colony in Saratoga Springs, New York. They had accepted me because of my first novel, and I went up there to try to resuscitate my failed second novel, *The Jewish Duke of Windsor.*

There were about twenty-five other people in residence, and it was the usual artists' colony assembly of writers, artists, and composers. In the evenings, after a hard day at our creative labors, we would often seek some kind of diversion, and one night, several of us went into town for dancing at a bar that had a jukebox. At twenty-seven, I was the baby of the group; the residents at the colony, for the most part, are usually in their mid-thirties to mid-forties, though there are always some youngsters and some oldsters.

I began dancing with one of the oldsters of our clan, Kaye. She was a lively sixty-four-year-old composer, whose hair was still blond. She was quite short, maybe five-foot-two. Short people, I've noticed, often age better than tall people because gravity has less to attack, and Kaye had bright blue twinkly eyes, a pretty face, and this really cute cleavage that she was always showing off by wearing

T-shirts and a push-up bra. Her breasts looked a little old and freck-led, but also firm.

A love song came on the jukebox and Kaye and I did a slow dance. She put her arms around my neck and pressed her lovely bosom against me. But that wasn't all that was pressing. Pushed into my crotch was something bulky and hard. Her T-shirts were always untucked, so you couldn't tell what was going on with Kaye below the waist, and I suspected that the solid thing I was feeling was a hardened upper-intestinal bloating-pouch, which I had often observed in most older people.

Nonetheless, we had a nice slow dance, and for a moment there seemed to be a current of Oedipal-sexual chemistry between us, but then the fast music came back on and the moment passed.

At the end of the night, when we all came back to the colony, everybody quickly dispersed to their bedrooms, and Kaye and I found ourselves alone together, having a cup of tea. She asked me if I wanted to go for a walk and look at the stars. Sure, I said. But before we went on our expedition to this one sloping hill, which was good to lie on and look at the wheeling of the night sky, we sprayed ourselves with mosquito repellent, which was necessary because of some recent rainfall.

So then we went to the hill and lay side by side and took in the hundreds of stars. It was quite romantic, and after a few minutes of feeling some unspoken tension between us—the taboo of it, our age difference—I eventually put my hand over her hand. And it's that first gentle yet courageous touch between a man and a woman that sets in motion this tumbling of events, like the workings of a clock. She squeezed my hand back, and then she explored my fin-gers and the strength and width of my wrist, my arm. Then in time I rose up and came down and put my lips to her neck, to the side of her face. And her arms went around me, pulled me in close, and we kissed. She felt small and fragile beneath me. She felt good beneath me.

But there was one thing wrong, and it wasn't her pouch. The smell of the mosquito repellent was very strong and acting like an antiaphrodisiac for both of us.

"I want to hold you," she said, "but this smell is too much. Let's wash it off."

I was staying that visit in my own private cabin, which had a studio for writing and a separate bedroom. It also had a bathroom with a large tub. So Kaye and I went to my cabin to wash off the bug spray.

She then suggested that we take a bath *together*, and with this woman thirty-seven years my senior, I got into that tub. I let myself look at her whole body only once. The pouch was for real; it was like a shelf above her vagina; it was like she had swallowed a brick. But she was so sweet, and as we sat across from each other in the bath, she took such wonderful delight in soaping up my penis, which grew quite large under her expert administrations.

"It's beautiful," she said. "I love it." And she was smiling happily. No girl my own age had ever seemed so unabashedly smitten with it.

So after our nice bath, we climbed all pink-skinned into my bed. We kissed and held one another, but because I didn't have condoms, we didn't make love. What we fell into was me curled up alongside her, sucking on her firm and wonderful breasts, which had good little nipples. And while I suckled, she was masturbating herself with one hand and masturbating me with the other. Occasionally, she would remove her hand from herself and put it on the back of my head, to encourage my nursing. It was all highly erotic. She was older than my mother.

And I was murmuring in my mind, "Mommy, Mommy, Mommy," which I often do, though, with women of all ages. But for me—someone who's had Oedipal problems his whole life—nursing on sixty-four-year-old Kaye was a great momentary resolution to the conflict.

So after about fifteen minutes of this breast-feeding, she began to come, moaning and gasping, and I was engorged in her tiny sunspotted fist, and at the height of her orgasm, she removed her hand from herself and put it on the back of my head and said so lovingly, breathlessly, "Oh, you dear boy."

And when she said "dear boy," it was like an electric cattle prod was put to my balls and the sperm shot out of me like a javelin. Normally it just kind of fizzles and burps out, but "dear boy" was so maternal that two nerve endings between my psyche and my testes must have linked up like two open wires, and the result was an ejaculation that went sailing over my head like a comet. Lord, it was spectacular. I only wish it had gone in my eyes and temporarily blinded me. Then it could have been the most Oedipal moment of a most Oedipal life.

Bald, Impotent, and Depressed

I USED TO BE A BREAST MAN, but now I'm an ass man. But I must qualify this—I like the ass, not the ass*hole*. That's too taboo. It scares me. Ta*boo!*

I still like to nurse on breasts, but it's more fun to nurse on the buttocks. They're like really large breasts. Also they have such a beautiful curvature, especially if you can get your lady friend to bend her knees while lying on her stomach. Then the ass is in the air and quite firm and delicious. The ass crack is also very nice, like a cleavage from heaven. So, in essence, if I am to be honest with myself, I must still be a breast man. I now simply pretend that the buttocks are breasts. There is the nipple problem, though. No nipples down there. That's why I haven't given up on the breast entirely. Regardless, it's all madness. I should be out discovering the North Pole, or doing something decent with my life, but instead all I care about is sex and my financial problems. And what about my soul? I hardly think of it. I need to pray more.

My problem is that I am surrounded by like-minded people—individuals who are obsessed with their genitals. For example, a few nights ago, I was at a dinner party in a dimly lit Tribeca loft. Halfway through the meal, my good friend Spencer, a therapist—

in-training, announced with pride that he had used Viagra. Naturally, the conversation up until that point had been about sexual intercourse—why women like to have their hair pulled had just been covered—but this Viagra confession shocked all of us.

"Why?" we all asked Spencer. After all, he's a young, healthy, vital man with a full head of hair and a good-standing membership at a sophisticated gymnasium.

"Well, it was the first night with someone and that's often difficult for me. I get stage fright. So the Viagra insured a good performance."

"It worked?" I asked.

"Oh, yeah," he said. "Nothing out of the ordinary, but it was very solid. No jitters. Viagra removed the anxiety."

"Won't you want to use it again? Might you not become dependent?" asked a woman at the table, a licensed therapist, who was pulling rank on Spencer, only a therapist-in-training.

"No," said Spencer, holding his ground. "I will only use it for opening nights when the critics are there. That's the only time when I might have problems. And now with this new woman I have established my capabilities as a lover. No having to prove anything the second night if I had been lousy the first night, which would make the second night worse than the first night. . . . So I advocate Viagra use . . . but only for the first night. Unless, of course, there's an emergency, and then one can keep the pill in a glass case and break it open like a fireman."

"Any side effects?" I asked.

"A headache. But who doesn't have a headache *after* sex?" Spencer lifted his eyebrow, indicating his utterance of a bad joke. And everyone found all of this amusing, except me. I felt betrayed by my friend. The whole world was going on Viagra. But I never will. I am against all pills and medications, anything unnatural. I have smoked crack cocaine, but I won't take antibiotics.

"This is terrible," I said to my dinner companions. "I won't go on Rogaine or any hair pills. And I won't take Viagra. I am a natural person. But I am going to be the only bald and impotent man in New York. I'll be completely alone."

"And depressed since you won't go on Prozac," said another friend of mine, a sculptor, and he laughed loudly as he said it, and everyone at the table joined him. My artistic friend knew well my legendary stance against Prozac despite my years of depressive episodes and suicidal ideation and compulsive masturbation.

"My God," I said, "I'll be the only bald, impotent, *and depressed* man in New York. I'll have to hang out in vegan restaurants. Only organically minded women will like me. I may become an acronym—a B.I.D. man."

After that there was a general discussion of who at the table had actually suffered from impotence. All of the men confessed to having had this problem at least once, though I've never really had this problem that I can recall, and needing to regain some stature with the ladies at the table, I said, "My problem isn't impotence, at least not yet. My problem is too many erections caused by too many things."

"What do you mean?" asked the woman therapist, putting me on the spot.

"He's polymorphously perverse," said Spencer, showing his superior that he has the goods.

"That's right," I said. "I've tried every perversion and none of them have stuck. I am now working on my soul."

Then the CD player went haywire, everyone made comments about CDs, and then the wineglasses were refilled, except mine, since I drink only temperance beverages. The evening wound down without further incident.

I walked home with Spencer. "I can see the future," I said. "I am going to need a woman who won't care that I can't get erections."

"There's no such woman," he said.

"I know one," I said, and I told him the tale of this lover I had on the Upper East Side in 1993. She was fifteen years my elder and we met in Carl Schurz Park while sitting beside each other on a bench. There was a sympathy in our worldviews and a two-month affair ensued. But she had a tremendous paranoia about venereal diseases, AIDS in particular, so she wouldn't engage in intercourse with me—she didn't trust condoms. She only liked to do one thing: sit on my face and suffocate me for about an hour. She was a tiny dark woman of Greek heritage and very demure, but she loved this dominant position. She said it made her feel like a queen on a throne. She wouldn't even move that much while I flickered my tongue and struggled for air. She even faced away from my penis, not very interested in it, and so without her looking at it, I could play with myself if I wanted. To her it was immaterial. After about an hour of just sitting there like a hen, she would have an orgasm. And the whole thing was so exotic and unusual that I enjoyed it.

This one time, though, there was a problem. She shifted her weight and my nose, which was buried, seemed to make a cracking noise. Then I thought I was having a bloody nose. I've been prone to bloody noses almost all my life. When I was seven years old, a mildly retarded, violent boy, who was eventually removed from his home and put in some kind of training facility, attacked me and smashed me in the nose, and I've had a weak vessel in my left nostril ever since. It's been cauterized many times, most notably when I really punctured the thing during that nose-picking incident when I was a teenager and almost bled to death.

Anyway, while my Greek lady friend was sitting on my face that one time when my nose cracked, I thought I was having a nosebleed inside of her. I began to panic. If this was the case, she would go insane. Bleeding inside her would be worse than coming inside her. Her AIDS paranoia was extremely severe. What to do? We were only about thirty minutes into our sitting. Naturally, I couldn't see what was going on. I was deprived of almost all my senses. It was an incredible predicament; I knew of no one else who had suffered a nosebleed during oral sex. And I didn't dare disturb my queen on her throne. It was a terribly long half hour that ensued. When her orgasm came and she removed herself, I ran to the bathroom, hiding my face from her. I studied myself in the mirror, and to my considerable relief, there was no blood coming from my left nostril, or the right. I had imagined the whole scary thing.

Spencer was quite impressed with this story, and I added that I was thinking of looking that woman back up. His therapeutic side emerged. "Listen," he said, "you can do better than a woman who just sits on you for an hour." Then he told me that a pretty woman at the dinner party, whom I didn't know very well, found me attractive.

"But I'm going bald," I said.

He ignored me and gave me her number. I called her and one thing led to another and by the second date I was in bed with her. And once our clothes were off, I immediately became overwhelmed with gas. I don't have erection problems the first time I'm in bed with a woman—I have gas problems. My nervousness produces flatulence. This woman was kissing me tenderly and I was trying to hold in farts. I excused myself from her bed to go to the bathroom. Luckily for me, the toilet had a fan, so there was no chance that she could hear what I was doing in there. I farted in safety.

I returned to her bed. A new fart needed to be held in. This was torture. Then the woman said, "I have condoms." The call of the wild. I tried to put a positive spin on things: I thought that my bloated abdomen might rub against her in a favorable way. I rolled on the condom, went to mount her, almost farted, and lost my erection. I rolled off her and removed the defeated condom.

"It's all this talk about Viagra these days," I said. "It must be subliminal marketing; it has destroyed my confidence. Please forgive me. This is my first experience with erection loss. With mild impotence." She was sweet and understanding. I let a fart slowly leak out. It didn't smell. To rally myself, I crawled downward and nursed on her buttocks. With my hand, I reached under her and tried to find the clitoris, but I couldn't locate it. I haven't been able to find one in years. But I was rubbing against the bed and an erection announced itself. I quickly put on a new condom. I mounted her from behind and was so nervous about the whole thing that I had a premature ejaculation. I tried to fake a few thrusts, but my spirit was crushed and the flesh was unwilling.

I rolled off. We lay there silently. Then I said, "My new book is coming out soon." I had to show her that I had some worth. She smiled at me in the darkness. Women are quite kind to men.

I didn't spend the night. I went home around two A.M. and called Spencer. He's an insomniac and can be reached at indecent hours.

"What happened?" he asked.

"She invited me up and I had gas. I got an erection but lost it. Then got another one, but I had premature ejaculation. My only recourse was to brag that my book was coming out."

The other end of the phone was silent. The study of object relations had not prepared him for this. Perhaps if he were a Freudian,
he might have been equipped to help me. Finally he spoke. "I can't
think of anything consoling to say."

"I'm going to call the woman on the Upper East Side."

"Good idea," he said.

Crack-Up

THE FIRST TIME I SMOKED crack was Christmas night 1992. The morning of that day, I had taken my six-year-old son and my parents to Newark Airport. They were flying him back to his mother in Georgia so he could be with her for Christmas. He wasn't able to fly by himself yet, and usually I flew him back down, but my parents were taking him this time, and after staying a little while with him in Georgia, they were going to visit old friends in Florida.

After I saw them all onto the plane, I drove back to the small furnished room I was renting on the Upper East Side, having moved out of Princeton a few months before to go to graduate school at Columbia. I was relieved that my visit with my son was over, but I was also devastated. It's the nature of part-time single parenthood. You fall in love anew with your child every visit; you give everything you can during this brief, intense period until you have nothing left; and then the child goes away and you return to your life, but you're emptied out, lost. You don't feel like a parent anymore, you don't feel like anything.

During this particular visit, I was with my son at my parents' house the whole time. Our schedule was simple: He'd wake around seven-thirty and we'd play all day until he went to sleep around nine. Sometimes my mother would take him grocery shopping, but for the most part I was with my son nonstop for two weeks. I was a young father, only twenty-eight, but my time with my son was exhausting.

When I got home from the airport, I immediately went to sleep. I woke up in the late afternoon and I didn't know what to do with myself. It was Christmas and my few friends were either out of town or busy with their families. Then I came up with something to do: I took the subway to Times Square.

I began in an Irish bar on Forty-third Street. I'm supposed to be sober all the time, but for several years I was periodically trying to see if something magical might happen to me and I could handle alcohol. I couldn't, but I kept trying. It's strange. I'm Jewish, but I drink like I'm half Irish and half Native American.

After a few drinks at the Irish bar, I walked down the block and went to Sally's, a transsexual bar across from *The New York Times*. I was new to the transsexual world back then; I had been going to Sally's for about a month, ostensibly to do research on a book I wanted to write.

There were only a few older queens at the bar—old in the drag world, that is; they were in their late thirties, early forties. They were survivors of the first wave of AIDS and they were like a strange, happy family gathered together for Christmas. They allowed me into their circle and I drank with them. I felt good. I told one of the queens, who was named Baby and looked like a Latin Elizabeth Taylor, all about my son. She bought me a drink and said, "You're sweet, *Papi*."

At some point I blacked out. I didn't fall off my stool, I just lost about an hour, and when I came to, a young black queen was sitting close to me and kissing my neck. I switched to club sodas for a little while and this young queen kept kissing me. She was nice-looking, thin, and she was wearing a black cocktail dress. For some reason she had taken a liking to me, and I was too embarrassed to ask her her name since I had probably been told it. The older queens were smiling at us, like we were some young couple in love.

I switched back to beer, and then the young queen whispered, "Let's go to my room and celebrate. I got some coke. Then we can come back here."

That sounded good to me and we put on our winter coats and headed out. It was around ten and I'd been drinking for several hours. We took a taxi to her hotel on Jane Street by the West Side Highway.

The hotel lobby was dirty and fluorescently lit, and an Indian clerk was asleep inside his bulletproof cage.

We sneaked past the clerk—if he saw me, I'd have to pay twenty dollars as her guest—but we stopped at the staircase, where there were boxes of canned foods, obviously left by some goodwill organization. My friend glanced to the cage—the man was still asleep—and she began to gather up some cans and asked me to grab some. "You can't be too proud when it comes to food," she whispered.

We took the cans up to her room, which was small and cold. There was no heat. We kept our coats on and she hugged me, part out of affection and part to warm up.

"Let's party," she said. "That'll give us some heat."

She got the coke out of her bureau drawer. But what she took out was a little plastic bag with tiny white pebbles inside. I had thought we were going to do lines.

"Is that crack?" I asked, scared and middle-class. She sensed my fear—the stigma that I associated with smoking crack—so she lied to me and said, "No, baby, it's freebase."

It was insane logic, of course—that freebasing wasn't as déclassé as smoking crack—but it was the kind of logic I needed in a flop hotel on Christmas night. And I knew she was lying, I knew it was crack, but I pretended to myself that I didn't. I thought how Richard Pryor had freebased and he was a genius, so it was okay if I freebased.

We sat on the edge of her bed and she took from her purse a thin glass tube about five inches long, with a piece of wire mesh at one end. "This is my stem," she said. She put one of the white pebbles on the mesh and put the other end of the stem in her mouth. She took a lighter, held the flame to the coke, and inhaled. The stem filled with a milky smoke, and there was an acrid smell, like the burning of plastic. She pulled until the stem was clear. Then she took the stem out of her mouth and her eyes rolled a little. Then she parted her lips and exhaled the smoke. She smiled like somebody relieved. She passed me her stem.

"I've never done this before," I said.

"You'll love it. But don't inhale. It's not reefer. Just hold the smoke in your mouth. That's how you get high."

I held the tube in my mouth and she sparked the lighter. I pulled down the smoke and watched it come at me. Then she took the tube out of my mouth and I held the smoke. Then I exhaled.

"How do you feel?" she asked.

"I don't feel anything," I said. I was embarrassed. I was a loser at drugs. She had me try again. This time it worked. It was like a soothing wash had been applied to my brain, my mind, my soul. A lifetime of anxiety was momentarily erased. I felt peace. And all over, too, there was this magnificent happy-sex feeling, as if the girl whom I had loved unrequited in high school had finally come up to me and kissed me with the sweetest kiss ever and told me she loved me.

We kept on smoking. I felt the smoke seeping through the roof of my mouth and going right to my brain. I gave my friend all of my money, around sixty dollars, and she went down the hall and bought more. We had no intention of going back to Sally's, and we smoked until it was all gone. We were out of money, so she searched the floor for crumbs. We smoked what was probably pieces of lint. Then we got under her blankets, still in our clothes because it was cold, and we held each other and rocked. She tried to touch me, and though I was still feeling sexy, I was numb down there, dead.

Then we both fell into some kind of hazy crack drunk sleep. When I woke up, it was four o'clock in the morning and I was sweating and panicked. I had to get out of there. I was in big trouble. She woke up.

"I have to go," I said. She could tell I was nearly crying.

"Don't freak, baby. I wanted us to have a nice Christmas." Her voice was pleading. She tried to hold me, but I got out of bed and put on my overcoat. "I can't let you go like this," she said. "Just wait. Sit down."

I sat on the bed and she grabbed a washcloth and left the room. The bathroom was down the hall, and she came back and put the damp, warm washcloth to my forehead. Then she bathed my face. In the midst of what felt like the lowest point in my life, she was kind to me. I calmed down some, but I still had to go. She let me leave. I never got her name.

I had one token in my pocket and I made it home, but I felt so fragile inside, like a wafer that could be snapped. On the answering machine was my son, prompted by his mother, telling me about his Christmas gifts. "I love you," he said at the end of his message.

I didn't feel much like a father, but I saved his message so that I would remember to call him back.

In a Dark Wood

IWENT ON AN EXCURSION to Fire Island with my friend the painter Harry Chandler, who is famous for three things: his ingenious paintings, his sexual exhibitionism, and his prosthetic leg.

Our trip to the island began at Penn Station early Sunday morning. While waiting for our train to Bay Shore and drinking two large cups of coffee, I noticed that there were many beautiful girls who weren't wearing bras. The shapes of their breasts were lovely and their little nipples looked so nourishing and inviting. It was incredible: just a layer of cotton between those nipples and the world.

I wanted to fondle myself right then and there, which has been happening all summer. I walk down the street and see all these lovely half-naked girls and I want to commit onanism every ten paces. It's maddening. But I don't think the solution is to cover women the way they do in Muslim countries. Rather, *I* should be blindfolded and given a Seeing Eye dog. I love dogs almost as much as I love women, and so I could play with my dog and take out my sexual frustration by wrestling with my canine friend.

"Look at all these girls with breasts," I said to Chandler. "What's going on here?"

"It seems to be a trend," said Chandler.

"I know. There didn't used to be so many breasts, but now they all want them."

We got on our train and we were both admiring a beautiful Indian girl, who looked to be about fifteen years old and had a luscious, swelling bosom.

"Like the many and varied spices that their land is famous for," I said, "I think Indian women are the most beautiful in the world because they seem to have the ingredients of every race."

"How so?" asked Chandler, engaging me platonically.

"Well, they have the delicate, birdlike limbs of the Asians, the handsome straight noses and high cheekbones of the Caucasians, the dark brilliant hues of the Africans, the chaste and mysterious expression to the eyes of the Middle Easterns, and the full hips and breasts of the Nordics. Yes, I believe Indian women are the most beautiful. I wonder if it's because of their country's geographic placement—the center of the world, the bridge between the East and the West. Or is it because they burn all the unattractive ones?"

"I don't know," said Chandler, and we both pondered in silence the profundity of my speculations. Chandler was wearing shorts and I glanced meditatively at his flesh-colored prosthesis, which goes from the knee to the foot of his left leg, and I wished I could strike his prosthesis with a stick of some kind to test it. "Where are the handsomest men in the world from?" he then asked, reviving our discourse.

"There's no such thing," I said. "All men are intrinsically ugly. That's why God created Woman, to compensate for the ugliness of Man. He screwed up with the first sex and improved with the second."

"Do you really believe everything you're saying?"

"I don't believe anything I'm saying. I only spit out what others have said and written, but in slightly different syntax so that it all sounds mildly original and we can pass the time pleasantly on this overcrowded train. You should know by now that I don't believe anything I say. How can I believe anything when I don't know anything? I only know one thing—I feel nervous most of the time. I am nervous, therefore I am."

The two cups of coffee were causing me to pontificate and I apologized to Chandler for this. He accepted my apology—he's very tolerant of me. Then across the aisle from us a fat man with a bald head began to kiss his chubby middle-aged girlfriend. I assumed that it was his girlfriend and not his wife because of the passion they were exhibiting. And it was uplifting to see two older members of society enjoying the pleasures of the flesh, but the man's kissing style was too much. His mouth was practically devouring the woman's whole face. "It looks like he's eating a piece of watermelon," I whispered to Chandler.

"You don't see that every day."

"You certainly don't. I may have to complain to the conductor."

Much to my relief, the two lovers eased up and ate bagels that the woman had packed. I stared at those bagels with envy. The two cups of coffee had dug a deep hole in my stomach.

So we made it to Bay Shore and then took a ferry to Fire Island. We were seated next to a nuclear family of four, who had a beautiful golden retriever. I nuzzled and made love to the dog and he responded happily, and his owners didn't seem to mind. The dog sported a pink hard-on and I sported one, too, but it was in my shorts.

We disembarked at Ocean Bay Park and went to Chandler's summer abode, ate a quick lunch, and changed into swimming trunks. Then we took a water taxi to Kismet, which has a famous nude beach. Chandler enjoys nude beaches as a healthy expression of his exhibitionism.

We looked for sexy women who we could sit next to and ogle, and we came across two gorgeous, sleeping lesbians—one was on her belly with her arm draped across her lover, who was on her back. We parked our blanket about ten feet below them. Chandler stripped down—I didn't look at his penis—and he ambled into the water, prosthesis and all. He's a graceful and courageous man.

I stripped off my shorts and lay on my belly. I looked right into the shaved genitals of the lesbian who was on her back. It was beautiful—like the folded, purple underside of a conch shell. The world at that moment was a place of great charisma and radiance. Chandler came and lay down next to me. We admired together that Sapphic womb.

After several hours on the beach—my ass got burned—we went back to Chandler's compound, which has clay tennis courts. We played two sets. I won 6–0, 6–1, though he does move exceedingly well for a man missing half a leg. Then I treated him to a $9.95 lobster dinner.

The next day, he had to work as an art instructor at the compound's day camp, and so I, following his suggestion, went to Cherry Grove, the famous homosexual community of Fire Island. Chandler told me that there was this primeval forest in Cherry Grove where men cruised one another. He had gone there and witnessed many incredible sexual acts. So I walked three miles along the beach and found these woods. It was frightfully hot and I was devastated from my march along the ocean because stupidly I had packed no water. So I staggered around in the woods on these sandy paths beneath the boughs of thick pines, and it was Eden-like in there, but I could hardly appreciate it—I was dehydrated and feeling hysterical.

I would pass men, but I was too scared to look at them directly. I wanted to witness sexual acts, but there was just a lot of staggering going on. Then I got lost in that shadowy yet hot forest, and I thought of Dante and *his* dark wood. And for the first time it occurred to me how my mother is named Florence, and was I always wanting to get back to her the way Dante wanted to get back to his Florence? Then I saw a pretty deer go walking by and I wondered if it was cruising for other deer. Then I worried about getting a tick.

All this thinking and cruising was very tiring, so I leaned against a tree, exhausted, and a man approached me. He mistook my heat prostration for a come-hither posture. He was short and dark. He wore sunglasses, covering his eyes, masking his soul. He went immediately for my nipples through my white T-shirt. What was the etiquette in such a woods? How to say "Hands off"? He found no reaction in my nipples; they are notoriously unresponsive. Then he made a grab for my cock, but it receded like a turtle's head. Disappointed with my lack of nipples and penis, he pressed on. With the dog on the ferry I got a woodie, but with the fairy in the woods, my own little dog hid like a pussy.

I made it out of there, and in a blind, confused state of dehydration, like Peter O'Toole in *Lawrence of Arabia,* I dragged myself for three miles on the beach and made it to Chandler's. He was back from camp, and after drinking directly from the tap, I told him what had happened. "No one ever touched me," he said, "but I kept moving. You really took a risk."

"That's because I have more homosexual tendencies than you," I said. "But those woods are dangerous. You can get Lyme's disease and VD all at the same time."

That night I returned to Manhattan, sunburned, but quite content with all that I had seen and done. I require varied stimulation. Then two days later there was my book party for my recently published novel. I wore my seersucker jacket (bought on sale in Princeton years ago, though I didn't have enough money at the time for the matching trousers), khaki pants, blue shirt, and my one Brooks Brothers tie. Because of all the sun on Fire Island I had a deep, reddish tan and so my bald spot appeared to be the same color as my hair, which gave to those around me the illusion that I had a full head of hair. Many people remarked on how young I looked. I knew it was the camouflaged bald spot, but also something about my book being published was having a slight Dorian Gray effect on me.

So the party, held in Turtle Bay Garden and thrown by my generous and kind benefactors, was a smashing success—elegant, glamorous, and crowded. And my great-aunt Pearl was there (see *New York Times* article, opposite). She liked all the free food, and she was very proud of me. She said, "This is one of the happiest nights of my life."

The publisher dropped off thirty copies of the book for people to look at, and twenty-two were stolen, de rigueur at such events, but I also convinced eight people to buy the book from me at a discounted price of twenty dollars. Perhaps this was done in poor taste, but I have been living off that $160 for several days—eating out, taking taxis, and buying espressos. It's a glorious time in my life right now. I almost feel like I deserve to have $160 in my pocket.

PUBLIC LIVES

Book Has Extras

JONATHAN AMES was wearing a seer-sucker jacket, just like the hero of his new novel, "The Extra Man." And **BLAIR CLARK,** a former executive at CBS News, was denying that Mr. Ames had learned anything about "extra men" (a k a "walkers" who escort wealthy women to Broadway shows and dinner parties) from him.

The things they talk about at those midsummer book parties.

This one was set in a garden behind Mr. Clark's townhouse on the East Side. Mr. Ames wrote much of "The Extra Man" in an extra room in the house; he has known Mr. Clark and his wife, **JOANNA,** for nearly 15 years.

Mr. Ames's 84-year-old great aunt, **PEARL VINE,** has known him even longer. "He devoted a whole chapter to me and he makes me out to be much older than I am," she said. Mr. Ames laughed. "I've had a character in each of my books loosely based on my aunt," he said, "and they're always her age."

Drinking

IN 1994, I SPENT MAY and June in Saratoga Springs. I was lucky enough to go again to the artists' colony. I was supposed to write, of course, but I was also trying to use the place as a health farm. I was hoping to get sober, but I wasn't having too much success.

Saratoga is known for its track and for its water. The horses, though, only race the last week of July and all of August. So I didn't do any betting, but I drank the water—it runs year-round. In the center of town, near a grassy little park, there's a public spring. The water has a sulfuric taste and it pours out of two spigots twenty-four hours a day. It's supposed to be good for your digestion; I was taking it for that and hoping, too, that it was good for my liver.

The fountain is underneath an open pagoda, which provides shade, and there are several benches so you can sit and take your time while you take the waters. The basin where the water lands is stained a glistening orange color—the residue from the water's rich mineral content.

One day I went to the spring. I was sitting on one of the benches and I was just looking at the water and listening to it before getting my drink. I was resting from having walked into town. An old man was on the bench next to mine. He had already filled a dirty, plastic cup and he was taking sips. Beside him on the bench was a paper bag with a bottle of booze inside.

He was wearing blue sweatpants with white stripes down the sides, a dark blue cowboy shirt, and old black leather shoes. He had closely cropped gray hair and the pushed-in nose of a bum. Only bums have noses that have been broken more times than boxers. His nose was like a crescent moon—the cartilage in the middle was all gone.

I knew we were going to talk. In 1986, I spent the summer living on Chrystie Street in the Bowery and the bums there always wanted to talk to me, and I always wanted to talk to them. So I was waiting for this Saratoga bum to start, like waiting for a girl to smile to give you an opening.

He made his move. He pointed to the water and said in a raspy voice, "It tastes like shit, but it's done wonders for my stomach."

He took a sip from his cup and he patted his stomach through his cowboy shirt to show me how good the water made him feel. But his belly was swollen and misshapen. He had all the alcoholic symptoms. I stood up to drink and I said in a friendly tone, "I like this water. It wakes me up."

I ducked my head and drank a little. It was cold and the harsh taste was a shock, despite my having tried it many times. Then I took some in my hands and bathed my face and neck. Then I asked the old man, "What's the matter with your stomach?"

"Ulcers. Esophageal ulcers . . . from drinking." He bowed his head and then said, "I add my vodka to the water, helps it go down."

I dried my face with my shirt and I sat down next to him on his bench. Somehow we were already friends. He moved the brown, crinkled bag that held his vodka to make room for me. He poured some of the vodka into his mineral water. I played stupid, as if I didn't know about drinking, and I said, "But the alcohol is giving you ulcers. Why don't you just drink the water?"

"I'm fifty-nine. I'm on disability. I got money in the bank. . . . I'm ready to die. Ready to go at any moment."

What he had said was an alcoholic's explanation of why he might as well keep drinking: He could afford it and he was waiting for it to kill him. But there were pitfalls to such a plan. A Bowery bum once said to me, "Somebody's played a trick. I didn't expect to live this long."

The Saratoga bum drank from his cup. Then he said, "Know what happened to me yesterday?" I shook my head no and he told me what happened.

"I cracked a check for one hundred, and the first thing I did I went for a haircut to clean myself up." He pointed to his close-cropped gray hair, which I admired; it made him look tough. He continued, "Then I got a liter. That left me with probably eighty-five dollars. Usually I get a pint, but I thought I'd go home, not come back into town, and I'd need a liter. But I drank the whole thing here by the fountain and passed out on that bench." He pointed to the bench I had been sitting on at first. He shook his head with dismay. "I woke up in Saratoga Hospital. . . . Been there more than once. I came back here and my bike was gone."

"What about the eighty-five dollars, gone, too?"

"Yep . . . and I need to get a new bike. And I don't have enough money. I left it right here. And I leave my cup under that tree every day so I can get my drink." Somehow the cup hadn't been lost.

"What time of day did you pass out?" I was trying to imagine who would take his money and his bike. I was just a visitor, but Saratoga, in my eyes, was a pretty nice town. Bums in the Bowery got rolled all the time, but this was a town with lawns and mansions, the New York City Ballet in August. If his money was stolen, it had to be at night, probably by kids.

"I think I blacked out around three in the afternoon," he said. "I went for the haircut around twelve."

"What time did you come to?"

"At eight o'clock, in the hospital. Had to walk home, three miles. I live out in the hotel on Route Nine."

I was playing detective with no chance of solving the mystery of his bicycle and money, though I wished I could retrieve them, but I also selfishly enjoyed hearing the details of his story; it captured why I love bums: Things just happen to them. Crazy things. They're like the white spores that dandelions become. They're not really in charge of their bodies anymore. The wind just picks them up and carries them away. It's tragic and doomed, of course, but I envy the caprice of it, the total lack of control. They just drift and land. They're in the right place, they're in the wrong place. They see murders, babies born, car accidents, fistfights, first kisses . . . trucks roll over them, banks fall on them, they lose eighty-five dollars, they find a wedding ring in the gutter.

I stood up and took another drink from the fountain. I imagined it purifying me, helping me. I sat back down and I said to the bum, "Where are you from originally?"

"Tennessee. That's where I got involved with horses. That's why I'm in Saratoga. Came here four years ago and fell in love with the place. On my bike I can get anywhere in twenty minutes."

"What do you do with horses?"

"I'm a groom, train a little," he said, "but my arthritis is so bad, I can't even get under a horse." He bent a little and made the motion of getting under a horse and scrubbing. I imagined that he had washed thousands of horses, that he had gone to tracks all over the country, following the horses like following the circus.

Drinking more and more every year. But the way he pantomimed washing a horse was beautiful. He had done it so much that the motion had become something perfect.

Then he said, "I want to go to culinary school. I've done some frying at the track, but I want to be an institution cook. . . . A line cook has got ten waitresses yelling at him, there's a lot of pressure, but an institution cook, that's more relaxed. Cooking at Skidmore, that's what I'd like."

He had claimed he was ready to die, but he wouldn't be talking about wanting to cook if he didn't have some hope left. I wondered if I could help him. But who was I to try and spread any word about quitting drinking? I'd had a binge two nights before and tried to drive my car into Saratoga Lake, chickening out at the last moment. It was private, drunken melodrama, and I spent the whole next day vomiting. I knew I needed to quit and I knew there were ways to do it, and maybe since I was trying to quit, I could help this man— he was only fifty-nine.

But I dismissed the idea. I figured the best thing would be to treat him with respect and not insult him by acting like an old-fashioned Salvation Army member. I said, "I have to go, but it's been nice talking to you."

"You too," he said. And I got up and took a step away from him, but then I had to give it a try. I always have to do things one more time—like one last swim at the ocean. Or with this old man, always hoping for something miraculous to happen. It's why I bring a baseball mitt to baseball games; maybe I'll catch a foul ball, even though I've never caught a foul ball. I turned around and I said to him, "You ever think of stopping drinking?"

"No, I can't—" He looked down, shook his head, then getting some bluster up, he said, "I'm all right. . . . I just have to get a new bike."

"I know I'm young," I said, "but I shouldn't drink. I'm trying to quit. The other night I was driving drunk. I could have killed someone."

"That's why I use a bike," he said. "I'll never get behind the wheel of a car drunk again. Even if I got my license back, I'd never take one drink and get behind the wheel."

"That's good," I said, but I knew he'd drive drunk if he ever got a license or a car again. It was easy to hear him lying to himself, but it wasn't so easy to hear my own lies—I still had my car.

"Well, I've got to get going," I said. "So take it easy." I was giving up as quick as I had started. I just wanted to let him be.

"So long," he said.

I started walking away and then I turned back to him one last time and I joked with him, though my concern was real. I said, "You're not going to pass out again, are you?"

He knew I was kidding around. He smiled and said, "I only got a pint today."

The Mangina

FRIDAY NIGHT, I WAS SITTING in the lobby of this theater in Tribeca called the Flea Theater. I was there to perform, to do some storytelling. I was one of several acts; the show was already in progress. I wasn't too nervous sitting there—for the last five years, I've done a fair amount of performing. At least once a month, I get on some stage somewhere in downtown New York and I tell stories from my life. I'm not quite a stand-up comedian, though I do stand. If anything, I'm a stand-up storyteller. It's a nice sideline to go along with teaching and trying to make it as a writer. It brings in a little cash—not much, but a little. So Friday night, I was waiting to go on and my friend Chandler showed up at the Flea lobby and sat next to me. He's been to dozens of my shows.

"I go on in fifteen minutes," I said. "And thanks for coming. You didn't have to. You've heard me so much."

"I always like your stories," he said, and he smiled at me, but he didn't look well. His thin shoulders were hunched, and his face was drawn. I could see he was making an effort to appear otherwise— he was wearing a clean blue shirt and his short blond hair was parted, neatly combed. And his forty-year-old face is always handsome in a worn, *Grapes of Wrath* kind of way, but I could tell this night that he was troubled.

"Is something the matter?" I asked.

He looked at me, hesitated a moment, then said, "I might really be losing it this time."

"What's going on?" I wondered if he was having a relapse with his exhibitionism; it had been dormant, at least in its unhealthy expressions, for some time. When he's being healthy, he goes to nude beaches, like on my visit to Fire Island; when he's unhealthy, he goes to Dunkin' Donuts and sits on the elevated stools at the front of the store. He wears shorts and no underwear and hopes that women seated at the tables might glance up and catch a peek of his testes. I think the likelihood of this is minimal, so it's mostly just the risk that he is probably drawn to. "You haven't been going to Dunkin' Donuts again, have you?"

"No, it's not that. . . . I've been making vaginas for two weeks," he said. "It's all I've been doing."

"What do you mean, 'making vaginas'?"

"Sculpting them out of this stuff called friendly plastic. It's this great material that I was using with the kids this summer."

"Sounds very pleasant—*friendly* plastic."

"You can do anything with it. . . . It's perfect for molding—I've come up with twelve prototypes for a prosthetic vagina. I come home from bartending and I'm obsessed. All I do is make vaginas—experimenting with flesh tones, hair. I finally got it right—a realistic-looking one. I put it on last night and walked to the Now Bar because somebody wrote a letter to you in the *Press* saying that's where drag queens go on Thursday nights. I figured I would show the drag queens the vagina and they might want to buy it, order one for themselves. But I went too early, the place wasn't open yet. So then I walked back home and the vagina was pinching me a little and then it started raining and my foot was creaking. I thought, I'm walking around New York in the rain with a squeaky foot and a vagina on. I must be losing my mind."

"You're not losing your mind," I said. "You're an artist, you're passionate."

"This isn't just about art. I think there's a lot of money in it. I just have to market it right. . . . I need the money. . . . A lot of men will want to buy a vagina."

This part *did* sound nutty to me. I didn't mind him making vaginas, but get-rich-quick schemes always betray mental imbalance and desperation. I had to disabuse him of this money angle, bring him back to reality. "Listen," I said, "there are already a lot of fake vaginas on the market. I've seen them where they come built into a pair of panties."

"Mine is different," he said. "I utilize my scrotum as labia. I have to show this thing to the world. I showed my roommate, but she screamed. I'm all alone with this vagina project."

"This sounds interesting, using the scrotum," I said. "You'll have to show me after my performance. So don't worry. You're not alone with this anymore. I am on the case."

Chandler smiled, reassured. It was time for me to perform, and Harry took a seat in the theater and I did my shtick. I hustled and hammed it up for the audience. Told three of my usual stories and plugged the book. A night's work. Then a jazz band came on and Chandler and I slipped out and walked over to his place, just a few blocks away, also in Tribeca.

We went into his bedroom, which is mostly his studio, and I said, "All right, let me see you in this vagina." I sat at his cluttered drafting table and he started getting undressed by his bed. I turned my back to him to give him some privacy. I was skeptical that his sculpture would look like a real vagina.

"It's on," he said, and I turned around and he ambled toward me completely naked. His vagina was mildly grotesque, but also quite authentic appearing. It was furry like a pussy and, sure enough, hanging out of a disguised hole was his excess scrotal sack, looking like puffy labia. He had the whole thing fastened around him with an extremely thin, clear tubing.

I was stunned on many levels. His body is sallow, boyishly hairless, reed-thin and yet muscular, though he has a slight paunch above the genitals. It is a handsome yet tortured body—from the left knee down is his rubber, prosthetic leg with its flexible rubber foot. So to see a vagina on this physique was rather remarkable. I felt both pity and awe. I was glad he was my friend.

"This is really good, Harry. It's amazing. You really are a great artist."

"Now I have a prosthetic vagina to go with my prosthetic leg," he said. "And I've built a fake hand I can wear."

"You're like that guy in the Dustin Hoffman movie *Little Big Man* who kept losing parts of his body. . . . You know, your scrotum really does look like labia. How does the rest of your penis feel?"

"It's not bad. I've put felt on the inside, so it's pretty comfortable. It's kind of like wearing a baseball cup. I want to call it the Mangina."

"That's a good name for it. . . . Where are the other vaginas you made?"

Chandler brought over to me a plastic bag and dumped out all the failed vaginas on to his drafting table. They were various shades of pink with differing amounts of hair attached (Chandler had taken the hair from real-hair wigs).

"Here's one without hair, for a shaved look," he said, pointing out to me a very pink Mangina.

"You've done a lot of work," I said.

"I think I was obsessed because it's a new way for me to exhibit myself. All these years, I've been wanting to show my testicles, but testicles are ugly. But a vagina is not ugly. So wearing this vagina, I can exhibit myself and not feel like I'm hurting anyone."

"So you want people to see you in this?"

"Yes."

"Do you want to dress as a woman, too?"

"No, I just want to be a man with a vagina sometimes. That's why it's the Mangina."

"Let's go visit my friend Lulu," I said. "She'll look at you. She'll love it. She's a beautiful transsexual and very wise."

"I didn't show you that I can finger myself," said Chandler, and he pushed his finger into his scrotal labia and it disappeared.

"Maybe there is money in this," I said. Then I called Lulu and I told her about the Mangina and she said we could come over. Before we headed to her place, Harry showed me a video he shot of himself. You can only see him from the waist down, and he's wearing the Mangina and lazily playing with his labia and then inserting his finger.

"This is completely depraved," I said, deeply impressed. "This makes Karen Finley look like a rank amateur."

It was only a two-minute video, and then Chandler got dressed and we took a taxi over to Lulu's, and when we got there, she was wearing a tartan skirt, stockings, and a white blouse. As always, she looked quite beautiful. She is elegant and tall and her skin is a lustrous dark brown. She was born in Africa and raised in Paris. She is a dress designer, with a steady, private clientele of queens and downtown divas.

I introduced these two good friends of mine, and then Lulu graciously offered us a choice of beer or apple juice. Chandler and I, both having no head for booze, opted for the apple juice. On the

TV, playing silently, was the David Bowie classic, *The Man Who Fell to Earth*.

We sat there drinking and I said to Lulu, "Wait till you see this vagina Harry has designed. It's a work of art."

"Please show it to me," she said.

So Harry went to the bathroom and stripped down. He came out shy yet happy. He loves to be seen naked.

"Oh, my," said Lulu, laughing. "What have you done?"

"You should touch it," I said to Lulu. "It's very realistic." I hadn't had the courage to touch it myself, but I knew Lulu was much more liberal than I. Harry stood right in front of her, and she touched his labia.

"This is warm," she shouted. "It's real!"

"Can you believe it? It's his scrotum."

"Your finger can go inside," said Harry, and he demonstrated this. Then Lulu put her finger inside.

"This is really something. You should have a show, a performance," said Lulu.

"Let's go to Edelweiss," I said, "and show the girls there Harry's vagina. He needs to have people see this."

The three of us left Lulu's and took a taxi to Edelweiss. It was midnight and the place was quite crowded. The owner's lawyers had somehow got it opened up again at its grand Eleventh Avenue location. We went to the large downstairs bar and Lulu pointed out queens whom she thought would be receptive to seeing Harry's Mangina. I'd then approach the queen and say, "I don't mean to be rude, but my friend Harry here is a crazy artist and he's sculpted himself a vagina that he's wearing. Can we show it to you?"

About five queens agreed to look at it, and we'd take them to this semiprivate corner of the club. Harry would then drop his pants and they all found the Mangina fascinating. At one point, a beefy security guard came our way—it's his job to make sure that no one is having sex—and I explained to him the situation and he shone his flashlight on the Mangina. The guard smiled and laughed, and the queen who was checking it out, a blonde, who's actually had *the surgery,* said with good humor, "Why did I bother spending twenty thousand dollars?"

Then it was getting late, so Harry and I said good-bye to Lulu—she was staying on—and we took a taxi downtown. We were both kind of quiet, spent from our exertions. I stared out the window of the speeding taxi—I was in a contemplative mood—and I took particular notice of all the Korean markets with their brightly colored displays of fruits. They were beautiful, but who would eat all those grapefruits and oranges and watermelons? It seemed to me that most people ate poorly and those fruits wouldn't move off the displays, the way one's novel (like mine) might not move off the shelves of bookstores. And then I thought how my novel, like a fruit with its bright green cover, and all the real fruits in New York would go to a terrible waste. I pitied myself and the owners of the Korean markets. But I had to not indulge in such thoughts, and the best way out of self-pity is to think of helping others. I looked at my friend Harry on the other side of the car seat. I had an inspiration.

"You know, Lulu is right," I said to him. "You *should* have a show. Maybe you *can* make money. Sell the Mangina as an art object. I want you to come onstage wearing it at my next show, which is October seventh at the Fez. I have the club to myself the whole night—no bands, just me. You can talk about the Mangina and then hand out cards with your number and people can order one if they like, or come to your studio and see your paintings. You can promote everything you do. Are you free on the seventh?"

"I am," said Harry, excited.

"Well, if it's a hit, since I'm the impresario, I'd like a ten percent commission on every Mangina sold."

"All right . . . Maybe to help sales, I'll play my accordion and dance."

"No, just come out there and stand in your Mangina. That should be enough."

"You're right," he said. "My accordion hangs low, might block the view."

"And the Mangina deserves to be seen! On October seventh, history will be made!"

Chandler smiled at me. I had truly come through for him, and I felt better, too. He wasn't alone with this anymore.

On October 7, 1998, as I predicted, history was made. That night, during my storytelling show at the Fez, the legend of the Mangina was born.

After my own ritual dance to Serge Gainsbourg's "Comic Strip," and a few introductory remarks, I asked Chandler to join me onstage. I had a good crowd, about one hundred and thirty people, and Harry was hiding in the wings. When I called him to come join me, he was brought out by my gorgeous and statuesque friend Gigi. I wanted him to be accompanied by a lovely woman to lessen the audience's shock and so that they wouldn't have a knee-jerk politically correct response to Chandler's Mangina—"How dare a man wear a vagina! It must mean that he hates women!"

Gigi, I figured, was perfect for the job of Mangina escort—she's an artist and also a world traveler and an expert on the unusual behaviors of primitive tribes. One of her claims to fame is that she rolled around on the jungle floor and made out with a cannibal in Indonesia who had shaved teeth. She showed me once his handsome, smiling picture. The teeth were very pointy and brown. "You could have cut your tongue on those teeth," I said. "I was careful," she said. "How was his breath?" I asked; the coloration of his chompers and the nature of his diet had me concerned. "Fine," she said.

So I felt that Gigi was the right woman to accompany Chandler and his Mangina. She's been to the heart of darkness and found love there—thus the Mangina wouldn't scare her, and her lack of fear and horror would be transmitted to the audience. It may seem as if I was being overly cautious, but I was going to have to perform after Chandler's appearance and I didn't want the audience to be killed.

So Gigi led Harry onto the stage and he was completely naked, wearing only his prosthetic leg and homemade, prosthetic vagina. Gigi discreetly walked off and Harry was showered with loud applause and lots of happy gasping. He stood beneath the lights and smiled sweetly. His two passions were merging—exhibiting himself and exhibiting his art. As the applause quieted, he began his speech, in his signature sincere, humble tones: "My name is Harry Chandler. I'm an artist and an exhibitionist and an amputee. I'm also a live Jonathan Ames story, which is not easy, let me tell you."

Unfortunately, no one laughed at that last line. It seemed scripted, which it was. Not by me—by Harry—but with my ego-gratified approval. Oh, well, that is the nature of theater—the occasional flat moment. So then Harry talked briefly about his career as an artist and his love of nudity—his own nudity and that of others—and how this love of the naked form led him to create the Mangina. Also, he disclosed that there was an emotional element: "My girlfriend left me," he said, "and I became obsessed with sculpting vaginas."

He showed the audience the various early prototypes of the Mangina and described at great length the various materials and elements he uses—friendly plastic, paint, wig hair, crushed velvet and elastic velvet.

Of course, the material that really sets the Mangina apart from other prosthetic pussies is one's excess scrotal sack, which Chandler pulls through a hole in the Mangina and utilizes as labia. He now calls this new organ the Lotum. This is a better mixing of the two words (scrotum and labia) than his first name for it: scabia (with a hard *a*). Lotum, he feels, implies something beautiful, because it sounds like lotus. And one of the benefits of the Mangina, Harry explained to the audience, is that he can expose himself in an attractive way, since he perceives a man's testes to be unattractive and a woman's labia to be attractive. I tend to agree with him, though there are countless others who must certainly prefer the scrotum. Also, I think that one shouldn't forget that there's a penis lurking somewhere in this whole thing, but Harry doesn't take the penis much into account, since it's mostly his balls that he was always trying to expose.

So Harry went through all the Mangina prototypes—they were piling up beside him on the stage like grotesque fish carcasses—and his lecture was getting a little tiresome, but there was no way for me to politely interrupt him. I couldn't give my own friend the old vaudevillian hook, but just when he was on the verge of really going on too long with his Mangina lecture, he finished up and I rejoined him onstage. I announced to the audience that we would do a little dance to celebrate our friendship. In my mind, I wanted us to appear like the naked women dancing in the circle in the Matisse painting, but I didn't tell this to the audience. The image, I hoped, would be subliminal.

So the Gainsbourg came on again and we held one another and hopped around. Harry did quite well with his fake leg, and a friend of mine told me later that the image of a naked, one-legged man wearing a Mangina and holding hands and dancing with a nicely dressed man in jacket and tie (me) was a great moment in performance art. "A new low," I said with a puffed chest to my flattering friend.

After the dance, Harry departed to wild applause. I was a little concerned that the night had reached its climax, but I began to tell my stories and the audience reassured me with their enthusiastic laughter. Though midway through my first story, my "Dueling Yentas" tale, in which I become a yenta, three people in the front row got up and left. It was rather ungracious of them, but luckily I was in character and so I verbally chastised them in my yenta accent: "Who are these terrible people? How rude! Who needs you, anyway. Now I'm all alone, I'm always alone. No one calls. No one cares. You three are horrible, selfish. Get out of here!" And so they slinked off, and I carried on—a pro, a trooper.

The night came to an end and I stayed onstage to peddle copies of my novel, and Harry was up there to show people the Mangina prototypes and the Mangina he was wearing. He was outfitted in this blue, long-underwear jumpsuit, which unzips down to the crotch, enabling him to quickly and efficiently expose his prosthetic genitals. This outfit is now called the Mangina Suit, and he looks like a superhero in it.

The two of us were quite happy up there on the stage—we were surrounded by females. Women began to finger Harry's Mangina, which he was loving, and cute girls were buying copies of my book and looking at me, I felt, with a certain adoration. An attractive brunette said I looked like Santa Claus—I was sitting on a stool, signing books propped on my knee. So I said to her, "Why don't you sit on Santa's lap." So she did, and she had a great little ass, but I had used up so much energy performing that I didn't get an erection when she sat on me. My penis was gelatinous and dead, almost liquid. I was mortified. I had a female fan on my lap and I might as well have been wearing a Mangina. I'm sure she felt how liquidy my penis was, but she didn't seem to mind, she slid off me smiling. I wanted to give her rear an affectionate pat as she walked away, but I wasn't sure this was appropriate, and my confidence for pulling off a rear-smack was feeling a little limp because of my limp penis, and then she was gone.

Then a blond girl took my hand and held it for a rather long time and took her other hand and put it on her attractive breast and said, "Your story about your son touched me *here.*" I wanted to touch her *there,* and then she, too, was gone. Gone. Into the night.

I wish these groupies would linger. I wish I could take a whole group of them back here to my apartment and look at them naked. They are all so lovely and different. I'd kindly ask them to strip and then I'd line them up against my wall. And while still wearing my jacket and tie, maintaining my dignity and not frightening them, I would study them and memorize their beauty.

When the memorizing was done, I would begin with the girl on the far left and first kiss her left breast, then the right, each time taking the nipple in my mouth like it was the most glorious pink grape, and then I'd go down and kiss her sweet triangular mound of sex—completing the triangle of kisses. Then I'd move on to the next girl and do the same. My wall can accommodate about six girls—if I move my sitting chair—which is probably six more than the number of groupies I have, but it's fun to fantasize that one has groupies. And for some reason, in this little fantasy, I need to have myself moving from left to right—my brain must be structured that way from all my reading and writing.

Then after all the tender kisses, these girls would surround me and hug me, and I'd smell their hair, their different perfumes. And I'd have some kind of spiritual and physiological eruption while still wearing my khaki pants because, as I envision all this, there's no intercourse. That seems too personal and brutal and selfish. Lately intercourse has been striking me as brutal, which is all right if you're brutalizing a friend. That's why men and women get together. The woman comes to trust the man enough to allow him to rape her but not hurt her, and the man comes to trust the woman enough to rape her but not be accused of rape. This is called a relationship.

But these fantasy groupies are strangers and I don't want to take advantage of their sweet attentions, I just want to be surrounded by their love and be petted and then have an orgasm in my underwear. Also, it's hard enough to please one woman, let alone six. And if I failed to please them, then they would no longer admire me—I would fall off my pedestal, off my authorial stool and seat of power.

But enough of the inner workings of my immature and lonely mind. After everyone left the club, Harry and I went upstairs to the restaurant above the Fez, the Time Cafe, and we had tea. He was subdued, and I felt my usual postperformance emotional devastation, but I fought it off. We recapped the night and compared notes; we were trying to suck a little more glory out of the whole thing.

"This blond girl was really fingering my Mangina," Harry said.

"Really? I think that was the same blonde who was touched by my story."

I felt a pang of jealousy that Harry got fingered by the girl, but I let it go. "Well, we made history," I said. "Beginning with the one hundred and thirty people who were in the audience tonight, word will spread rapidly about the Mangina. It will be whispered everywhere on the streets of New York. Your fake lips will be on everyone's lips. Once a thing becomes a word, it is alive, real. This is my prediction. Not too many people invent something worthy of a word. You should be proud, Harry."

"The Mangina now has life of its own," he said solemnly, almost sadly.

"A life of its own," I said. And we sipped our tea.

All I Had in Me

I'VE ONLY SLEPT WITH one postop transsexual. This was a couple of years ago, back in February of '96. I was on a real bender. It began when I had to meet this editor at the Rainbow Room. The fellow was interested in my work. My head was still shaved back then and I felt funny going to the Rainbow Room with my shaved head. I was being let out of Brooklyn, where I was living off my credit cards to pay for my room right next to the BQE. The damn Robert Moses BQE, which sliced through my Navy Yard neighborhood and made me seasick for two years, rocking my bed, rocking my desk. But the rent was cheap. But not cheap enough. There had been cutbacks, and so I only taught two composition classes at my business college, which didn't cover the rent. It didn't cover much. Except maybe the hundred dollars I ended up giving the woman, the postop transsexual.

So it started at the Rainbow Room with this editor. He was a sweet guy, a little fey. A little gay. A nice face. A nice smile. We got a table right next to the window. It was like flying over Manhattan in a plane. It was decadent. So much money. So many lights. So much fear of the dark. So many buildings. But I did like it; I was charmed. Schoolboyish.

"It's beautiful," I gushed. "Like a man-made Grand Canyon. God. New York. What a city." What a dope. Me.

"You've never been here?"

"No."

"I love taking people here for the first time," said the editor. "It's the best place in the world to get drinks." The waiter, a stern mortician of a fellow, came over.

"What would you like?" asked the editor. The waiter waited.

"I don't know," I said. Did I risk taking a drink? This was business. If I drank, I could really screw up. I was trying controlled drinking at the time, which meant not doing cocaine. "What do you think I should have?"

He looked out the window. "Let's have Manhattans," he said.

"Of course," I said. This time I'll drink like a normal human being, I told myself. Also I'd never had a Manhattan and I was curious. In my drinking life, I hadn't ordered too many fancy mixed drinks. For the most part, I stuck to beer and wine. If I drank hard liquor, I tended to black out too quickly because I drank so fast and mixed drinks are small but potent. Wine and beer come in larger glasses and I could enumerate them with some control. Two bottles of red. Twelve bottles of beer. Those were numbers I could handle, keep track of.

The Manhattans came. Mine was delicious. I tried to pace myself. I drank it in two minutes. "Can I have another?" I asked the editor, like I was Oliver Twist. "I've never had a Manhattan before."

"Sure," he said, and he smiled. I drank the next one in five minutes. We mixed in a little talk about the book I was working on. "Can I have another?"

"Maybe you'd better go slow," he said. "But okay."

I drank the third one and then a fourth. He had half of a second one, and by then we weren't talking about my book. I pressed my face against the window. "I'm drinking you, Manhattan!" I shouted, and I was laughing.

Then I was crying, going on about life and how everything is loss and how I desperately miss everyone who has ever left me, and the editor was completely charmed by such sensitive emoting. When I'm sober, I have no affect to my personality, but when I'm drunk, I'm this maudlin clown who loves everybody and laughs and then weeps and then vomits and blacks out.

We were there maybe an hour, and when we left, I remember thinking I might throw up during the high-speed descent of the elevator, which would make me seem like an unreliable writer, a bad business investment. So I held down the puke, and then the cold, fresh air of the street steadied me. It was February. The editor hugged me good-bye.

"You're so much fun," he said.

"Thank you for the Rainbow Room and all my Manhattans."

"I never saw anybody drink like you," he said and laughed. It was all fun and funny for him.

"I do the best I can to please," I said, and then he hugged me again and was off. Nine months later he rejected my novel. That's all right.

So I staggered down Broadway and I picked up four women hairdressers from Puerto Rico. They wanted me to take their picture. They were in town for a hairdressing convention at the Javits Center. After I took their picture, I said, "Come drink with me." And because they weren't Americans and they had some soul, they came with me. I took them to a Mexican restaurant on Forty-third, which I thought they would like since they were all a little homesick, not liking the cold. And it was only later that I remembered that Puerto Rico wasn't in Mexico. I bought them margaritas and I had beer. Then they bought the next round, and the ones after that. We took more pictures, mostly of me squeezing and hugging them. I grabbed a lot of good plump ass. They let me get away with it.

"My own Mexican harem!" I bragged, and they laughed. Their English wasn't that good, so they probably thought it was their fault that I was referring to them as Mexican. Who knows. At some point, I left them, thinking there was little chance they'd invite me back to their hotel room for an orgy, so I kissed them all good-bye and stumbled for blocks down to Eleventh Avenue. To Edelweiss. All sad roads lead to Edelweiss.

One of the girls there, a friend, gave me a joint. That stabilized me, probably kept me from blacking out. And I felt that marijuana was okay, as long as I didn't do cocaine. Cocaine meant utter devastation and having to go home and live with my parents. It had happened before.

So I bellied up to the bar, had another beer, and peered down at this short girl standing next to me. There was something about her that seemed authentic.

"Are you a real girl?" I asked.

"Can't you tell?"

"I can't tell anything anymore."

"I'm not like the girls in here. But I used to be. I had surgery."

"Oh," I said, and I was intrigued. This was my first time meeting a postop transsexual, and I had always wanted to ever since I was an adolescent tennis player and Renee Richards (formerly Richard Raskin) attempted to qualify for the women's draw at the Forest Hills U.S. Open.

"If you want to fuck me, it's a hundred," she said.

She looked pretty good in Edelweiss's shadows. "All right," I said. Our negotiations may have been a bit more protracted, but that was the essence of it. When we got outside, under the streetlights, I saw that the face was brutal, almost simian. One must always take the lighting into account at Edelweiss. But it was too late; it would have been rude to back out.

She had a car and we drove to a cash machine. I removed the hundred, half my life savings. But I figured it was an investment, that I was sure to write about whatever happened. So here I am getting the money back, with interest.

We drove to Queens, which was upsetting. Whenever I go with prostitutes to Queens, I feel guilty. My great-aunt lives there and she's lonely. So I feel that if I'm in Queens I should see her, but I'm usually whoring around after midnight, which is too late for a visit. Not to mention that she would disapprove of my behavior, especially my wasting money when once in a while she sends me a check. I do love my great-aunt. Who else loves me enough to just give me money? My parents take me in, but they never just give me money.

So I shoved my guilt about my great-aunt down in my liver, with all the other poisons, and the postop queen and I went to her apartment, which was quite nice. She lived much better than I did. She made a good salary as a secretary, but I gave her the hundred anyway. A deal is a deal. We went into her big bedroom and in the corner was a child's pink bicycle. Turns out she had a kid, a little girl, from when she was married as a man, and the girl came to stay with her on the weekends. I was up to my neck in pathos and it only got deeper.

We smoked a fat joint and climbed into bed. She wanted to keep the light on. I wanted to shut it off, but I didn't want to hurt her feelings. The light stayed on. The face was rough, but the marijuana helped a little. She lubed herself up. Put a condom on me and lubed me up. I mounted. The hole was tight. But not like a woman. Just a hole. No changes in temperature. No variety of tightness. A hole in her body. But I worked her good. Grabbed her hard, fake boobs. Looked at that face. Managed to stay erect. She sucked on my mouth with her mouth. I was drunk. Stoned. I pumped.

"Tell me I'm your girlfriend," she whispered hoarsely.

"You're my girlfriend."

"Tell me you like me."

"I like you." Who was paying whom?

"Tell me I'm pretty."

"You're beautiful."

"Tell me I'm your girlfriend."

I obeyed all her wishes. And I worked. I pumped. I'd catch glimpses of that little pink bike. My heart was breaking. "You're my girlfriend." I said it without her asking. I kept fucking.

"Slap me," she said. I reared up and slapped her. It made me come. We smoked another joint. The marijuana did something to me. I mounted her five times. The hole never felt good. Her face was a mask. I left at six A.M., asked for twenty of the hundred I gave her so I could get a taxi on Queens Boulevard. She gave it to me. I had earned it. She asked for my number; I wrote it down. She gave me her number.

I slept the whole next day. Woke up once to vomit. She called me that night. "You made me feel like a woman," she said. "Most of the time, I feel like it's a big mistake. But you made me feel like it was worth it. Please call me sometime."

"Okay," I said. We hung up. I never called her. For one night, I had saved her. That was all I had in me.

Oy, Oy, Oy

I NEEDED TO GET OUT of the city. Everything was becoming Mangina this, Mangina that. All people wanted to talk to me about was my friend Chandler's invention of a prosthetic pussy. I was a guest on a late-night, call-in radio show, and even there the whole discussion revolved around the Mangina. At one point, I screamed into the airwaves, "I'm a serious novelist, not just a pitchman for the Mangina."

Luckily, at the height of this Mangina mania, I had a reason to leave town—I had to give a reading at a Midwestern university. So I was very grateful on late Monday afternoon when the car service came to take me to La Guardia and thus out of Manginattan.

Unfortunately, the automobile reeked of lemon-scented disinfectant. Car-service cars always smell like peep shows, like the swill they mop up the semen with. And I wondered if it was dangerous for my driver to breathe in this toxic, fake lemon odor during his long shift. He was a nice Haitian man and on his dashboard was a series of four photos of his pigtailed, young daughter. As we were stuck in brutal, soul-destroying traffic on the BQE, I imagined that he must look at her pictures during such jams and think, I'm doing this for you.

He deposited me at the airport and after a brief wait it was time to board my plane. I got to walk on the tarmac and I felt like an old-fashioned, intrepid voyager. But then I saw my aircraft—it was a petite, thirty-seat affair. I suddenly wasn't so intrepid. It looked like the kind of small plane that when it exploded only made back-page headlines:

COMMERCIAL CRAFT GOES DOWN IN MIDWEST,

KILLING THIRTY

The seats were cramped, and once the door was closed, there was a terrible smell of bad breath. The whole plane, because it was tiny, reeked of someone's stale breath. First the lemon smell in the car and now acidic halitosis. My sensitive nose really does work against me, making my life a purgatory of odors.

To make matters worse, it was a rocky, horrible flight. I prayed agnostically that my life would be spared and was greatly relieved when we landed. Then I was met at the gate by a nervous and eager graduate student in the writing program. He was holding a sign with my name on it.

"Put that away," I said, referring to the sign. "I'm Jonathan Ames. We don't want to alert the paparazzi." The young fellow had red hair like my son and he blushed as we shook hands. After all, he was meeting a visiting, published author from New York City!

We walked out to the parking lot. It was late, around ten P.M., and we had an hour's journey ahead of us. He wasn't a bad driver and I only feared for my life once or twice. Naturally, we talked about writing.

"I'm taking all these feminist-Marxist theory courses," he said. "I think it might be screwing me up. But the teachers here are into theory."

"Don't listen to them. Theory for a writer is like saltpeter for a soldier. If you have to appease your teachers, just put a woman Communist in one of your stories, that should be enough."

"What's saltpeter?"

"You know theory, but you don't know saltpeter? They sprinkle it on the food in West Point, it cuts down on libido. I'd like to get my hands on some."

"Some of the other graduate students told me you write about sex a lot. I apologize, but I haven't read your books. I will very soon. They also told me I should bring you a bra when I met you at the airport." He kind of giggled; he was trying to be risque with the published, perverted novelist.

"A bra! Those impudent snots. I will have to lash them tomorrow. Point out these scoundrels. . . . But it's interesting this using of a bra to tease me; there seems to be a trend developing. My character in my novel has bra trouble, and some prankster recently mailed me a bra without a return address. I'd like to find out who did this."

I looked out the window; the Midwest was very dark and my thoughts were dark—I try to create literature and I'm sent anonymous bras. I moved the conversation off of writing.

"I feel very Jewish out here, away from New York City," I said. "It's a good thing I left my yarmulke back home."

"I don't mean to frighten you," he said apologetically, "but the town next to the school has a big headquarters for the KKK."

"That's all right, I belong to a Jewish terrorist group. These people don't scare me."

"Really? The JDL?" He was naive and decent.

"Oh, no, it's called the Oy, Oy, Oy. We infiltrate organizations like the KKK and the neo-Nazis with an undercover, subversive agent—a worrier. Notice the similarity to the word *warrior.* And this worrier then transmits profound anxiety and insecurity into these groups, destroying their confidence, Yiddifying them, and making them less prone to violence."

He was a good sport and laughed, though I was a little concerned about wasting such material on him. We kept up our chitchat, and then, finally, we arrived at the campus. I was being housed in the former residence of the college president. It was a beautiful nineteenth-century home, now used for visiting dignitaries. But I was to be all alone—I was the only dignitary on campus. The young writer gave me a set of keys for my room and then said, "I have some beer and pop for you in the trunk."

I knew I was far from the land of the Mangina when he said *pop.* I thanked him for his thoughtfulness, but refused both the pop and beer and urged him to keep the refreshments for himself. He seemed disappointed. I think he was hoping I would invite him up to my room to share the six-pack and he could then have the full experience of hanging out with a *writer.* But my dipsomania has been in remission for almost two and a half years, since the spring of '96, and I couldn't risk drinking a beer—I didn't want to go berserk so far from home. I told him I'd see him at the reading and we wished each other a good night.

My room was lovely, old-fashioned. My bed was an antique—a four-poster affair with a canopy. I slept well and in the morning after a shit, shower, and shave, the three essentials, I was met by the writer who had invited me to this Midwestern U. He's a tenured professor in his mid-forties, a former New Yorker. We got in his car and he took me to a bakery for coffee and a muffin. He laid out my agenda. I was to sit in on two of his classes, then there would be a dinner followed by the reading.

"For dinner," he said, "we'll go to the one place in town where we can get a martini." Everybody wants to drink with the visiting writer on these junkets. "Joining us will be my colleague, Professor K." He paused, to let this information sink in. "I understand you know his daughter M."

"Oh, God!" I exclaimed. I hadn't seen M in four years. I suddenly remembered her telling me about her father who taught in the Midwest. Was there no escaping myself? I had come out to the land of the neo-Nazis and blue cornflowers and the KKK, only to be forced to have dinner with the father of a girl whom I used to ravage and shtup quite nicely.

"He wants to meet me?" I asked. "Is this a good idea?"

"He read your book and liked it very much. He doesn't seem to harbor any ill will."

"It *was* a nice relationship, but usually fathers don't like to meet ex-boyfriends. Oh, well, it's a small world."

I sat in on the two classes and eyeballed all the girls. Then free of obligations for a few hours, I walked around this beautiful American campus of oak trees and brick buildings and long walkways. Everyone was wearing down vests and jeans. I was in my Nabokovian Professor Pnin costume of tweed coat and corduroy pants. Leaves were falling, the sun was bright. . . . I'd follow one pretty girl and then pick up the scent of another. It was the land of blondes, and they all smelled like shampoo. It was delicious. I really wanted to defile someone.

Then I went back to my room to rest up for the night's events, and I wished I didn't think about sex so much. It's so demanding and tiresome. If only I had money and could really travel, I could get my mind off of fornication. But traveling to college campuses only fosters thoughts of humping.

So I lay under my canopy and thought of M. I remembered fondly her ass and gently spanking it. Why do I often spank women? I suddenly wondered. Am I that patriarchal? I wondered if *I* should read feminist-Marxist theory. But I slapped away that train of thought and visualized a naked M. Then I nobly fought off the urge to masturbate, not wanting to weaken myself before a public appearance. I always treat my readings and performances like a boxer in training for a big fight—don't jerk off! So I napped and then my colleague collected me around six to take me to dinner, where I met Professor K, M's father. He was perfectly gracious and we got along very well. The two professors had martinis and I had club soda. K, I noticed, had M's eyes, her best feature. It made me miss her.

Then the reading went off all right, there was a nice crowd. When I finished, I saw my grad student friend from the night before and he had a copy of my book for me to sign. I dispatched him quickly, hoping pretty young coeds would approach me, but the mild homoerotic quality of what I read must have scared them all off. A gross disappointment. What's the point of giving a reading at a college if you don't get laid?

So I went off with six male graduate students to a bar and watched the Yankees win game three of the World Series. Yet again I did not drink, which seemed to sadden the young writers. I can only hope that their next guest writer will be an alcoholic who actually imbibes.

After the game, I walked back across the campus alone and happened to peer in a dormitory window. I saw a girl in panties and a T-shirt climb into the top bunk of a bunk bed. The panties were light blue. The ass was beautiful. I was pierced with desire. Then that desire immediately turned into depression. It had nowhere else to go. I staggered through the leaves back to my antique bed. I thought of the girl in the blue panties, and I felt old and ridiculous and sad, and for the nine millionth time in my life, I masturbated. How much do I have left in me? How much longer can this go on? Instead of crying, I keep ejaculating. Just once when I'm sad I should cry myself to sleep, try something new.

Then that night I actually dreamt I was wearing a Mangina. My body was still in the Midwest, but my subconscious had obviously returned to New York.

The Lord of the Genitals

I'M AT THE ARTISTS' COLONY AGAIN. I've been in residence a month, and it's beautiful here on the edge of the Adirondacks—the air fresh with the end of fall and the coming of winter—but a few days ago I was overtaken by a sickening depression and I felt like I was losing my mind. But a girl with an ass like two delicious hams saved me.

The depression started one day when this very famous older writer and I went to a racquet club to play tennis. He had just finished reading my novel, which was very generous of him, and as I drove us to the club, he told me that he liked my book very much, and then he asked, "Do people think you're gay?"

"I don't know what they think. It seems to be my great strength that I appeal to all sexualities, which I imagine is very good for sales."

"You should try to make your next book more heterosexual," he remarked, which was not out of line. He's in his late fifties and he is allowed to dispense advice. He is a master of the novel and has had numerous best-sellers.

"I've thought of trying to write more heterosexually," I said. "It would really confuse people. Also it could help me get laid. But I'm currently working on this trilogy—you know, like what Henry

Miller did, and J. R. R. Tolkien. It's called *The Lord of the Genitals.* And the first book isn't very heterosexual, I'm afraid. It's called *Cocksucker.* The second book, though, *Pussy-Licker,* is quite heterosexual, and so is the third book, *Ass-Eater."*

The older writer seemed intrigued, and as we had a fairly long ride to the racquet club, I committed the cardinal sin of telling another writer what I'm working on.

"The whole trilogy is about this one guy, a writer, named Amos Nathan," I said, gripping the steering wheel as we careened on back roads through pine-covered forests. "In the first book, *Cocksucker,* the one I'm working on now, he's down and out. Broke. Depressed. Living in Brooklyn. And when he has no money and he's feeling suicidal, he has a yearning to suck cock. Specifically the cocks of young Puerto Ricans. He finds it incredibly humiliating yet erotic to have their penises in his mouth. Though after a few minutes, he also finds it boring. But somehow this cocksucking keeps him going, it's his only connection to people. And it's practically heterosexual cocksucking, because he sometimes thinks of the penis as an enormous, comforting, substitute nipple, especially since he's too down and out to attract any women. But ultimately the penises are not comforting enough, and that book ends with him attempting suicide.

"But he doesn't kill himself, and in the second book, he begins to have some success—he sells a novel—and he starts getting women. And he goes through a real pussy-licking phase. Can't get enough of it. All he wants to do is lick pussy. Just loves to be down there, their legs around his head, their juices going up his nose, his hard-on grinding into the bed, though after thirty or forty minutes of licking them, he does like to mount them and copulate.

"Then his book is turned into a movie by Hollywood and he becomes really successful and gets even more pussy to lick. So it takes a Fitzgerald-like turn, and it ends with his soul being corrupted by too much pussy and Tinseltown.

"In the third book, *Ass-Eater,* he meets a Danish actress in Hollywood, and one night while licking her pussy from behind, he eats her ass. Actually he licks it. But I don't want the third book to be *Ass-Licker* since the second book is *Pussy-Licker.* So he licks her ass and he loves it. But he finds that he only loves to lick the asses of Northern European women. No other kind of asshole does it for him. It has to be German, Norwegian, Danish, Icelandic, or Swedish. Even the Belgian ass is too southern for him.

"So he gives up Hollywood and moves to Stockholm, where he can have an endless supply of the right kind of ass to lick. His descent into decadence is complete. But the cost of living is very high in Stockholm, and so Amos, after two years of only licking asses and not writing, goes through all his money. He loses everything. It's obviously a moral tale.

"And when things get really bad for him, it happens to be winter, and because there's no sunlight that time of year in Sweden, he becomes more depressed than he's ever been in his whole life. But there are no Puerto Rican cocks for him to suck, which might have kept him going for a little while, at least until the sun came back, and also he doesn't have enough money to fly back to the States, and so this time he does successfully kill himself, becoming another Swedish-winter suicide victim. . . . I see the trilogy as an homage to Goethe, Selby, Hamsun, and Goldstein."

"Goldstein?"

"The publisher of *Screw.* Do you think anyone in the United States will publish this if I actually see my vision through to the end? I was thinking I could at least get it serialized in *Screw*—that's why it's an homage to Goldstein—or my own paper, the *New York*

Press. But the *Press* doesn't serialize. I could slip the chapters in as columns; I'd be serializing and they wouldn't even know it."

"That's not a bad idea—serializing. I see it as a salacious twenty-first-century Dickens or Twain. They both serialized a great deal."

With that we pulled into the parking lot of the racquet club and played three enjoyable sets—I thrashed him rather mercilessly. As an adolescent, I was something of a tennis whiz. Town champ in '78, though my nascent tennis career was cut short in 1979 by my well-documented puberty problems. So it's nice as an adult to get to employ the old serve-and-volley.

But the next day, despite the good tennis, I was too depressed to work. By telling him the whole plot and scope of my masterwork, I had shot my wad. There was no need to write the thing now. It had lost its mystery for me. And I had given it to him on a silver platter, so now he was going to write it, steal it.

That night at dinner I eyeballed him. He had been destroyed by me in tennis, and he had acted like he took it well, but writers are a ridiculously competitive lot, so he would exact his revenge by robbing me of my trilogy. I was sure that he was already hard at work on his version of *Cocksucker.* What had I done? I could hardly eat. He was sure to finish before me. He's written dozens of books. He could crank out *Cocksucker* in two months. By the time I finished, if I even could after having ejaculated the story on him during the car ride, it would seem as if my work was derivative of his.

So after dinner I read over the fifty-odd pages of manuscript I had, and in an irrational fit I threw it all into the fireplace, and then erased what was on my computer as well. It was all the writing I had done since coming to this damn colony.

That night I hardly slept, and the whole next day, I wandered through the woods talking to myself. I was deeply depressed. I felt my brain slipping out of its casing and down my neck, like an egg sliding on a frying pan.

So I skipped dinner, unable to face the other residents of the colony, especially the famous writer. I got in the car and went into the small town, to a diner, and then to a café. There I came across the free alternative weekly of the nearest city, Albany. In the back of the paper, just like with the *Press,* there was an adult section. Salvation! Sex listings!

Prominently advertised were these places that offered private lingerie modeling. I called one of them and received directions. It's one of the forms of prostitution—usually found in the American hinterlands—that I was aware of but had never indulged in.

It took me about forty-five minutes to find the lingerie place, which was called Tres Joli and was located near a small airport. Houses of deviancy, I find, are often near airports. I guess the rent is cheap, and the location is remote, which is good for husbands not wanting to be spotted by family and friends.

Tres Joli was in a white, aluminum-sided, one-story shack with an empty gravel parking lot. The little house was quite dark when I approached—it was around nine o'clock at night—but I fearlessly rang the bell.

I was greeted by a gorgeous blonde in a bikini. She led me into a small reception room that had a display case filled with dreary, cheap lingerie. Another bikini-clad woman, a brunette, came into the room.

"You're here for a modeling session, right?" asked the blonde.

"Yes," I said.

"A half hour is forty dollars, fifteen minutes is twenty-five. Which would you like?"

It's always best to choose the lesser amount of time in these situations. When love is not involved, things quickly become redundant and a tad maudlin. "I'd like a fifteen-minute session," I said.

"Okay, which of us would you like? I'm Suzie and this is Carly."

I hate it when they make you choose like that. I wanted the blonde, but I didn't want to hurt the brunette's feelings. All night long she must have been passed over. I almost chose her, out of misplaced sympathy, but after a moment of awkward silence, I said, "You, Suzie." The brunette took it well and went back to the next room, where she plopped down on a couch and watched TV.

Suzie then led me to a small room with only an easy chair and a boom box. I paid her, and then she put on some music and began to dance for me. There was to be no lingerie modeling. That must have been some kind of legalism, a front. It was basically a place for private stripteases. On the wall was a sign that said, NO TOUCHING. And next to the chair, I noticed, was a big bottle of moisturizer, a box of tissues, and a little garbage can filled with *crumpled* tissues. They could have at least dumped that out. I wasn't supposed to touch Suzie, but I was expected to touch myself, to jerk off.

Suzie was about five feet eight. She had small but perfect breasts, sharp cheekbones, and natural silky blond hair. I engaged her in conversation. She was eighteen years old, enrolled at a business school, and was rather jaded. She kept encouraging me to get comfortable—which meant I should whip it out, but I kept it in my pants. And as she danced for me, I thought how not too long ago, she was just a girl. I was worried that by working in such a place at such a young age, it would be hard for her to ever fall in love, that she would think for the rest of her life that all men are fools. Then I remembered that all men *are* fools.

After that train of brilliant thinking, I then had my requisite spiritual crisis. I need more God in my life, I thought, not more sex.

Then I realized that sex does bring God into my life. I'm always praying to be relieved of sexual obsessions. So having worked that out, I began to enjoy Suzie. She stripped and everything about her body was great, but her ass was a revelation. Each cheek was like a big pink ham, and because she was eighteen, the hams were firm. It was miraculous. Watching her ass was like taking a yoga class. Time slipped away. I became completely relaxed. Before I knew it, my fifteen minutes were up. She walked me out and gave me a kiss good-bye on the cheek.

When I got out to the car, a little giggle rose out of me, from some lower chakra. My depression had lifted. My brain slid back up my spine and into my head. So what if I had given away *The Lord of the Genitals*. I had seen an ass for the ages. That's much better than writing a trilogy for the ages.

The Sex Card

THERE IS NO WRITTEN RECORD of the 8,764 (estimated) working erections I've managed while making love to women. And I'd like such a record. A decent sexual performance is one of the most heroic acts that an urbanite or someone not prone to real adventure can achieve in this life. There are so many obstacles, both physiological and psychological, that one must overcome to simply mount one's lover that such a thing should be acknowledged and kept track of. So what I'd like to have is a baseball card equivalent for my sexual performance. Unfortunately, my peak years have already passed, but I will start keeping track immediately, and perhaps the latter part of my career will be productive. Ted Williams, for example, kept hitting until the end of his playing days.

I'm going to call this record of my lovemaking achievements the Sex Card, and if this thing takes off and others are interested, I'll get Topps, the baseball card king, which already has a name loaded with sexual innuendo, to be a distributor of the Sex Card.

On the front of the card will be a simple portrait photo, nothing pornographic, a cross between a yearbook picture and a mug shot, and on the back of the card will be the categories in which performance is judged. Like a baseball card, errors and losses will also have to be acknowledged. But I hope that my card, once I put it all together, will be of all-star caliber and a statistical wonder. As a boy I loved to look at a star's baseball card, like Henry Aaron's or Willie Mays's. There was something magnificent about the consistency of year after year of strong, good seasons with beautiful numbers like 38 home runs, 123 RBI's, a .324 average. For me, there's a gorgeousness to good baseball numbers, and it's the most fascinating way to judge a man's life—his statistical output. So I want to have the same thing for the one area in my life in which I've put forth the most amount of effort—mounting women. And, too, I want to provide such a thing for my fellow men. There should be a card for women as well, but I will find a lady friend to come up with the female equivalent, since she will know better how women judge their own sexual performance. Also there should be a card for the gay community, and any other community that I can't think of at the moment.

The Sex Card, naturally, will be set up like a baseball card. On the top of the graph will be the categories, and running down the left-hand side will be the years—1999, 2000, etc. One's height, weight, age, and birthplace will also be put down. But I think penis size will be excluded, since surely lying will abound in this area and the whole validity of the card will come into question.

The first performance category that comes to my mind is what I will call the GHI—Gas Held In. So many times with women—usually during the first few weeks of our acquaintance, the time of seduction—I am overwhelmed with flatulence, such that I'm in a constant state of heroically recirculating and redirecting gas into other parts of my body. Often, when it seems I am just about to burst, I am able to suddenly channel a fart into some mysterious holding area—and who knows what damage is caused by this suppression—buying yet again more time to continue my seduction.

In such instances, I feel quite the superman, like James Bond deactivating a world-destroying explosive with only one second to go. And I feel especially proud of myself while under the duress of holding gas in if I am able to produce an erection, which is some kind of lower-body muscular feat. But I'm also terribly annoyed with myself that I'm so gaseous during these times; it's some kind of curse.

Why I produce so much gas during the period of courtship is an interesting question, which I should briefly cogitate on. I can no longer tolerate the word *intimacy,* just as I find vomitous the hyphenated word *self-esteem,* but I think my production of gas at the outset of relations with a woman is some kind of literal smokescreen to keep the woman away, to block intimacy.

(About intimacy—what a nice word destroyed by the New Age; and furthermore, I can't stand how all of life's problems in this New Age are related to self-esteem, specifically *low* self-esteem. What if self-esteem is found not to exist, that the concept is completely wrong, like the late-nineteenth- and early-twentieth-century psychiatric study of nose structure as a determinant of personality? What would those pioneering psychiatrists have thought of my long, bent, and bony nose? They would have classified me as someone sexually maladjusted and overwhelmed periodically by fear of things that are not fearful. Then again, nose study perhaps *is* good. In any event, I can't stand the word *self-esteem;* it's so limiting. The self is boring. I like to think of the soul. Much more interesting.)

So every time I am able to hold gas in, or have a GHI, I feel that I deserve credit for it. There can also be the flip side to the GHI, the GLO—Gas Leaked Out. I have to say that I've had very few GLO's. I usually steal away to the bathroom and pee and at that time fart as much as possible. Or when I leave a lady friend's apartment, I walk down the street and happily fart for blocks, and when

I do such a thing, I wonder how many of my fellow pedestrians are also wildly and clandestinely farting as I pass them.

On to the next category—the FTWE, or First Time Working Erection. This refers to getting an erection the first time you make love to a new lady friend. What a relief to actually have a hard-on when you need it—after all, the pressure is enormous on opening night. The flow of blood to one's brain, producing all that worry and anxiety, limits the blood flow to the penis, but if you are able to have enough blood to engorge the penis while at the same time being wildly self-conscious, then this should be noted on one's card—it's a great achievement. Then there's the APE, Avoided Premature Ejaculation, which doesn't need explaining. *But* I am extending the time frame on premature ejaculation: If that first time is to be considered a successful mount, for the woman to think there might be hope for you as a lover, you have to last more than five minutes. (This is a very low number, and as you sleep with the woman more and more, you should almost never have an orgasm before the eleven-minute mark, unless you are impressing her with the fury of a quick and sudden attack, or if it's decided upon beforehand that it's going to be a short one—like the two of you are heading out for dinner, but you want to do it quickly, that sort of thing. In general, I advise my friends that if they want to be considered good lovers, they should maintain intercourse for at least sixteen minutes, with twenty-four minutes as perhaps an ideal amount for a mount.)

Now, the flip side to the FTWE and the APE can be just one single category, the HE, Humiliating Embarrassment, which can be undone by the PYAA, Proving Yourself After All. I had a friend just recently tell me in an E-mail that the first night with a woman he couldn't get it up, but compensated like a champion with a healthy dose of oral gratification for the young lady, which could also be a category—OC (Oral Compensation). He then spent the night, another noble deed, and in the morning, he reported to me, he was able to successfully mount her and prove himself. And I feel that such a thing should be recorded! Hence, the need for the Sex Card.

Other categories will steal from the acronymic world of the baseball card: 2B, 3B, and HR will stand for, respectively, doing it two, three, or four times. And you can get credit for doing it twice if one was at night and one was in the morning. That shows a healthy ardor and should be noted. Doing it five times is enough of a rarity not to warrant a whole category, but can be mentioned at the bottom of the card in a little sentence: "On September 23, 1989, Jonathan made love to a woman five times over the course of three hours!"

And then there will be categories that acknowledge producing a climax in a woman: OBI (Orgasm By Intercourse), OBM (Orgasm By Mouth), OBH (Orgasm By Hand), and OBOT (Orgasm By Other Thing, such as a slipper or a belt buckle). And one last category—there should be one for decency of mind—the ACONPS, Acceptance Of Non-Playboy Standards, which can be very difficult for men brainwashed at an early age by airbrushed pornography. Other categories to consider could be the CL, Clitoris Located, and the NCM, No Condom Mishaps, but I am worried that the card not be too cluttered looking.

Now, not having any precedent for a statistical year of lovemaking, I'm not sure what will constitute a good season—thirty GHI's or fifty? Twenty-four OBM's, eight PYAA's, and thirty-six OBH's? Regardless, keeping track of my sexual performance will be a worthwhile endeavor, and I am curious to see how I will do this season.

Well, I think that just about covers the Sex Card, and so I must end this discussion—also, life is intruding. I am currently stationed in New Jersey at my parents' house, where I am with my son for the next three weeks, during his long Christmas vacation, and he just came in and asked for breakfast and I quickly tried to close this document on the computer. I didn't want him to see what his father was writing, but he managed to see "Non-Playboy Standards" and laughed. Then we ended up just now having a sexual-education conversation. He took from my windowsill, where there are various odd knickknacks, a little square cardboard condom holder. It was one of those novelty condoms that you get in toilets in bars across America. Someone gave this condom to me years ago and stupidly I never threw it out. This particular novelty condom claimed to be fudge-covered. My son sat down on my bed and studied the condom package and said to me, "Me and my friend found a whole roll of condoms in this abandoned truck. It was sick! We set one of them on fire. The thing really burned."

"Playing with matches. That's not good," I said, though it intrigued me to imagine a burning condom. I then decided I should tell him how to properly use a condom, rather than setting one on fire. "Let's open this condom up," I said, "and see if it's really fudge-covered."

We opened the thing up and there was no fudge on the red condom that emerged from the little box. "What a rip-off," I said. "I guess it melted."

"'Keep at room temperature,'" my son read from the box.

"Well, let me explain to you how to use a condom," I said. "You unroll it onto your penis—"

"I learned this in the fifth grade and this year in the seventh grade," said my son.

"Well, some things are good to learn over and over," I said, and my son is certainly nearing the age when he might actually put a condom on. He's nearly thirteen, has grown two inches since the summer, reaching the height of five feet nine, and is sporting blond peach fuzz on his chin and upper lip. Also he asked me if we can rent a movie he spotted at Blockbuster, *Breast Men*.

So I unrolled the condom and put it on my index finger. "Now, after the condom is on, you then put your penis inside the woman and move around and it feels good for you and for the woman." I made an upward motion with my condom-covered finger to demonstrate penetration.

"I don't need visuals," said my son, properly chaste.

I continued with my lecture, without further hand gestures: "And the condom, when you have an orgasm, prevents you from getting the woman pregnant and also protects you against any sexual diseases that could be exchanged."

"Sick!" he said to cover up his genuine, burgeoning interest. I took the condom off and threw it away. My son then stood up and launched an attack on me. My life with my son is like a *Pink Panther* movie. I'm Inspector Clouseau and my son is the Chinese manservant. He is always leaping out of doorways and giving me karate chops to the neck, and stuffed animals are always falling on me from door frames. And when secret attacks aren't launched, he's like this enormous young bear cub always wanting to engage me in wrestling and finger fights and tickle fights (he looks like a teenager but is still very much a little boy).

So after I threw the condom away, he lunged at me and went to grab my fingers to bend them back, but I bent his fingers back, and even though I was causing him mild pain, he was giggling madly and then he tried to bite my wrist. He's always trying to bite me when we have these finger fights, and it has me mildly concerned.

"No biting!" I shouted. I fought him off for a good two or three minutes and then pleaded, "Let me just finish writing and then we'll have the whole day together. I'll make you some eggs, then we'll go for a hike, it's not too cold. Then we'll go to the Y and play basketball, and then tonight we'll rent *Breast Men.*" This final supplication seemed to get through to him and the attack came to an end.

Well, as I finish up here at my desk and happen to glance at the discarded condom in the garbage can to my right, I think of the sex lesson I just taught my son and I worry about his future. I hope he won't turn out too troubled because of me. I hope he manages to have a good sex life, a good life. I hope he's a Ken Griffey, Jr., to my Ken Griffey, Sr. I hope he's a better player than his dad.

The Mangina Is Optional

I HAVE ONE CHAIR and I was sitting in it. I looked out the window. The sky was gray and lifeless, edging toward end-of-the-day darkness. And all the chimneys were smoking, exhaling white clouds, heating up apartments for people coming home from work. It was like a bunch of old men puffing on pipes. It was lovely. And I was lonely. I was afraid. But afraid of nothing. No one was coming to get me, but I often feel like they are.

I got out of the chair and into the bath. Soothed my asshole with the warm water. I need baths. My asshole needs baths. I felt better lying there. Wished I wasn't so scared of life half the time. Scared to live. Scared to die. But it's a good thing we die. Otherwise there'd be no urgency. No reason to do anything. There's hardly any reason now, but we've got to fill up the time. Like reading before going to sleep. You need to do something before it's over. And then there's the heart. We love. We love other people. That keeps you busy. But it's also what makes the dying terrible. I don't want anybody to die. I'm afraid of them dying. So baths are good. You're suspended. Warm. Your asshole stops burning with fear.

I got out of the bath and got dressed. Jacket and tie. The works. Then winter coat and hat. Then I grabbed my suitcase filled with my props and headed out. The sky was black now and I walked down First Avenue to Performance Space 122, to my off-off-Broadway, one-man show of storytelling—*Oedipussy.*

On the way, I passed the old, wildly stooped man who prays to Virgin Marys wherever he can find them. This time he was praying in front of the Mary painted on the wall by Ricky's, the odd little gift store on the corner of First and Third. I like Ricky's. I go in there sometimes to look at the Richard Kern book of naked girls or the little Taschen erotic-photo books.

And the old man, the Mary worshiper, I've also seen him many times up on Second Avenue, stooped in front of the Spanish church, looking in the window at the Virgin there. He holds on to these metal bars and you can just see the icon through a sliver of glass, surrounded by her red candles. He stares at her so intently, his lips moving with words, his posture that of someone pleading.

I also saw him in front of another church, again because of a Mary, but I can't remember where. And he's always immaculately dressed—jacket and tie and hat—though his shoes are worn down since he has to drag them. He's horribly bent, like a crooked finger, his chest parallel to the ground, a caricature of curvature, of old age. So he leans on his aluminum cane, shuffling from Virgin to Virgin. But I don't know if she's doing him any good. He looks more frightened than me, unless it's the pain from his back that contorts his face with worry. And it's kind of a paradox, but he's so pious-seeming, one wonders why he needs to pray so much, but then it's all the prayer that makes him holy. Though maybe he's praying because he's burning with guilt from some terrible misdeed, a guilt so burdensome he's bent in two, or perhaps he is holy after all and is simply praying for others. I'll try to think of him that way from now on.

So I passed him in front of Ricky's, and when I got to Fourth Street, I thought, Five blocks to go, and at Fifth Street, I thought, Four blocks to go. Then midway between Fifth and Sixth there was a crowd of people hovering in front of the two Indian restaurants, which compete with each other by seeing who can have more Christmas bulbs in their windows and on their walls and ceilings. And usually I don't mind people, but this crowd annoyed me profoundly. When I'm on my way to my show, I can't stand it when human beings clog the sidewalks or stop suddenly in front of me. I want them to behave like cars. I wish people had directional signals on their hips. If they're going to stop, they should signal and then pull over to the side. Too often they stop in the middle of the sidewalk, oblivious to me, and give no directional or flash any brake lights. Out of my way, you idiot, I think privately. But I only have such thoughts when I'm expected somewhere nerve-racking, like a performance. And here in front of the Indian restaurant was this ridiculous gaggle of twenty-something fools, happy and talking, excited to eat Indian food. All the boys still had hair on their heads, and all the girls still had nice asses in their jeans. I had to go into the avenue to pass them. Rude young idiots, I thought. I couldn't even take pleasure in the girls' asses.

Then between Sixth Street and Seventh Street, my mood was vastly improved when I passed a good-looking dog, a dark brown Lab. We locked eyes for a moment—two lovers from a former life reunited—and I felt quite happy. A good omen for the show. I love dogs. Just their gleeful eyes can turn my whole spirit around.

At the theater, I set up my stage and then annoyed this fine fellow, Ben, who runs the lights, by telling him, like I do every show, that I was scared and didn't want to perform, and then I went out to get my coffee. I almost always go to the Bendix, but before two shows I went to the Korean deli on the corner of Ninth and both those shows ended up being bad. So, like a baseball player, I must observe my superstitious rituals. Thus, Bendix coffee in hand, I returned to the dressing room, thirty minutes before curtain. I then endured the terrible preshow process of peeing and shitting several times. I have found out that I am not alone in this need for constant evacuation right up until the moment one goes onstage—a fellow P.S. 122 performer says he goes through the same thing.

But I can't stand all this peeing and shitting, especially the shitting. I worry that I won't get everything out of me, and if I'm onstage and still have something in my intestines, maybe I won't perform well. But also by evacuating so much, I worry that I am losing all my *chi*, all my energy, out of my ass.

I go onstage at seven thirty-five, and it was about seven-fifteen on this particular night and I was taking a break from the toilet and just sitting there in my dressing room staring at the mirror. I was filled with self-doubt. Why do I do what I do? Why do I tell everyone these stories from my life? Why do I make a clown of myself? Then I heard footsteps on the back stairs that lead to the dressing room.

"Mangie?" I called out. Mangie is my tender nickname for my one cast member, my good friend Harry Chandler, known to many now simply as the Mangina, in honor of his wearing his prosthetic vagina, which complements his prosthetic leg, which he must wear, though, unlike the Mangina, which is optional.

"Yes, Jonathan, it's me," he said, and then he was in the room and sat down next to me in front of the long horizontal mirror. We looked at each other in the glass. It was a solemn, quiet look. We both made morbid, sad clown faces. The minutes before a performance are like the minutes before an execution.

"What are we doing, Harry?" I said, breaking the silence. "We are making fools of ourselves."

"I know," said Harry. "It's penance for all our sins. It's 1999, we've got to do something. All those years I was trying to get women to look at my scrotum in sneaky ways, and now I'm out there humiliating myself . . . a man trapped behind a Mangina. The Mangina is my penance."

"Yes, you're like the man behind the iron mask, but instead you're behind a plastic vagina."

"But on the positive side, I think it's a joyful penance," said Harry, "because I'm atoning and people are laughing."

"That's good. But what's my penance? I'm confessing all the time. But how can I atone?"

"Why don't *you* wear the Mangina?"

"No, that's not for me. . . . The Mangina is your cross to bear. Maybe you could make me a plastic dunce cap, except it would have a penis coming out of it. I would have to wear that for three months and be laughed at until I was humiliated to the point of being a spiritually pure human being."

"Do you want me to make it out of a mold of your penis or mine?"

"Mine, I guess. It's the one that gets me into trouble."

"That's why I think you should wear the Mangina. You can't get into trouble when you wear a Mangina."

Then this soul-searching conversation was interrupted by Ben. He poked his head into the dressing room and said, "About five minutes, Jonathan."

"Okay," I said. So I went into the bathroom and was quite at ease, and this is because I've grown ever closer to Harry during the course of *Oedipussy*, such that I am now able to sit on the toilet, which is only separated from the dressing room by a door, and relieve myself even while he's there. The first week of performances, I had to ask him to leave the dressing room, but now, like a lover, I don't mind if he hears me defecate. He's very tolerant. When you wear a Mangina, it makes you accepting of others.

I had what I hoped was my last bowel movement a little past seven-thirty and then came back into the dressing room and began to hop up and down to get warmed up. Harry was setting up his computer. He's backstage almost the whole show—until he comes out and shows the Mangina for two minutes—so he does computer drawings to pass the time. He's been doing a series of perverted portraits of me, all featuring my large beakish nose and thin hair, and now he was working on a design of my dunce cap.

"I'm going to give the audience their money's worth tonight," I said, trying to pump myself up.

"Yes, you will," said Harry, playing the loyal cheerleader.

I stopped hopping up and down. "I feel weak," I said. "I think I've left my show in the toilet." I then cupped my hand and held it under my ass so that no more *chi* could fall out.

"What are you doing?" asked Harry.

"Making sure no more energy falls out of my ass."

"You eat too much gluten," said Harry, who's very anti-gluten. "And you eat in restaurants too much. That's your problem. You're loaded with bad restaurant bacteria, that's why you're shitting so much."

"I cooked at home today."

"Well, then I don't know what your problem is. I guess you're insane."

"Don't say that before I'm going to perform. And look who's talking. I'm not the one who wears a Mangina."

"That's so easy—make fun of the Mangina. Everybody turns on the Mangina. At first they like it and then they turn. I have no women. No family. Everyone rejects the Mangina."

"I'm sorry, Harry."

"That's all right. You're actually the only person who has stuck by the Mangina. Did I tell you my father sent me my birth certificate? He's disowned me. Thinks I've destroyed the family name by connecting it with the Mangina."

I put my hand on my friend's shoulder. Then Ben came into the dressing room and said, "Places."

It was a good show that night. My best one yet. It was a large, raucous crowd, and there were three pretty girls up front. They inspired me. I kept talking about my penis. I told the girls if they were interested they could contact me care of *New York Press*. They smiled. They smiled like they liked me. I can see them in my mind, sitting there, beaming. It's a sweet thought. I wish I could go back in time and get on my knees and crawl to them and put my head in their laps and look up at those smiles and ask them individually, "Are you my mommy?" Which is my way of saying, "Do you love me?"

So the show went well, I gave everybody their money's worth, and then Harry and I went out for dinner—my treat. Afterward we both felt sick.

"See, it's restaurants," he said.

"You're right," I said.

Then at the corner of my street we shook hands and said good night. But then I asked him, "Which leg is the fake one?" He walks so well with his prosthesis, just a slight limp, that you can't really tell which one he's dragging, and I always forget.

"The left one," he said.

I was feeling a little nutty, what with having performed and the nausea after dinner, so I asked, "Can I kick it?"

"Okay," he said. But before I could kick him, he swung his fake leg into my shin.

"That hurts!" I cried, and I limped around in a circle, trying to shake it off.

"That's the one advantage to having a fake leg."

"Well, I'm sorry I wanted to kick you. I deserve the pain," I said.

"You do deserve it."

"God, that thing is like armor. You really should make your whole body prosthetic, to go along with the Mangina and the leg. You'd be invincible."

Harry smiled. He liked the idea of invincibility. Then we shook hands again and limped off in opposite directions.

Epilogue

Of Loneliness and Dipsomania:
My Trip to Europe

OR YEARS I'VE BEEN COMPLAINING that I'm obsessed with sex because I haven't had enough money to travel. I kept imagining that if I did something decent, like see the world, I wouldn't be thinking all the time about women's asses and breasts and legs. Not to mention my occasional homoerotic fantasies where some man pistol-whips me with his cock—reveries brought on by an emotional longing for my father that I haven't resolved and perhaps never will.

So my mind is a sea of sexual stupidity and life is so short that there has to be a better use of my time. There are charitable actions I could take that probably would get my mind off of sex, but hospitals where one can tend to the suffering and ill are always overheated and this makes me very tired, and to be selfless and giving, you need energy. Thus for a long time I was always thinking that traveling was the only way out of the mental/sexual gutter. And then, sure enough, recently my prayers were answered: I was invited to come perform my one-man show, *Oedipussy,* in Germany. I was to be paid a handsome fee and provided with an open-ended round-trip ticket. So I left for the Continent on February 24, 1999, and had plans to travel for three weeks after giving my performance.

I packed lightly and simply. I took two pairs of pants, and everything else was in threes: shirts, underwear, T-shirts, and socks. I also
had my favorite mustard-colored Brooks Brothers sport coat, one
sweater, an overcoat, and four Raymond Chandler novels. But the
most important thing I packed was a bottle of psyllium fiber in cap-
sule form. I usually take powdered psyllium, but a large can of psyllium powder takes up too much room in one's bag, and also once
when I was visiting my son in Georgia, my can of psyllium burst
open and for weeks all my clothing had fiber on it. So I felt very
good that I would have my psyllium in Europe—no way did I want
to risk travel-induced constipation. I also packed a bottle of vitamin
C, my razor, toothbrush, and toothpaste. I figured I'd use hotel soap
for my hair and as shaving cream. Well, enough of that, but pack-
ing isn't talked about sufficiently in travel writing.

So on the afternoon of the twenty-fifth, I arrived in Heidelberg,
where I was to perform at the German-American Institute on the
twenty-seventh. My very first night in Heidelberg I ate in some
restaurant-bar, and while awaiting my food, I made this note in my
journal: "Beautiful, tall raven-haired waitress with khaki pants
wedged up her ass in a very attractive way. All of her is thin and
tall, except the ass, which is sumptuous. Banana-type breasts, high
cheekbones, taut skin . . . too taut, but oh, that ass. Very intriguing
the way the pants are sucked up into it. Well, food is here. Will stop
writing."

I offer this very first journal entry of my trip to illustrate that any
thoughts of freedom from sexual obsession were obviously hopeless.
Do I mention in my little notebook the fact that I had seen
Heidelberg's famous lit-up castle in the mountains just moments
before? No. I write with great rapture about a waitress's wedgie. So
for the rest of the trip, it was life pretty much as usual—thoughts

about sex around the clock, punctuated only by hunger and exhaustion and, because I was in Europe, the study of train schedules.

But I should say that I was able to look around me a little bit, and I noticed that Heidelberg is very beautiful, almost as beautiful as that waitress's ass, and the Allies didn't bomb it very heavily for that very reason. Unlike much of Germany, Heidelberg still has its prewar elegance.

A river, like in most European cities, bisects this old university town, and to the right and left above the town are two small mountain ranges. And on the face of the eastern hills is this glorious castle, which has enormous spotlights shining on it at night to give one the feeling that the Duke of Heidelberg is still up there doing romantic things, like having banquets and sword fights and orgies.

So I walked around lovely Heidelberg for two days and hiked in the surrounding forests, and then on the evening of the twenty-seventh, I had my performance and it was very well attended. The publicity had worked: All over Heidelberg there were posters announcing my show and those of my two fellow New York performers who had preceded me—Evert Eden and Penny Arcade. Under my name and the title of my show was the phrase *lust spiel,* which I figured must mean sex talk. But I was later told that *lust* meant comic, which leads me to wonder what the German word for lust is. I should have asked. Probably something that if directly translated would mean punctuality.

During the course of my show, I cracked several anti-German jokes, which the audience good-naturedly enjoyed. In the first story I told them, I was talking about my life-changing back spasm that occurred at that Cub Scout picnic in 1972, and how this spasm resulted in my wearing of a corset for a year at the tender age of eight. And I said to the audience, completely off the cuff, "I don't know what the German equivalent for Cub Scouts might be. Perhaps it's the Junior Stormtroopers or the Baby Luftwaffe." At "Baby Luftwaffe," they really laughed and I had them in the palm of my Jewish hand. And so I duly informed them that I was a Nazi, but not the kind they liked—I was an Ashke*nazi*.

Later in the show, I told them that if, God forbid, there was another Holocaust, I knew that they wouldn't use that shower trick again. They'd tell us Jews that we were going to watch a movie, since they know how Jews like to go to movies, especially on Christmas, and so they'd get us into some cinema and then the gas would come. To dramatize this, I then pretended to be choking on gas and cried out, "I thought I was going to see the new Woody Allen!"

At the end of the show, I received three encores, which gave me a chance to make meaningful eye contact with several blond maidens whom I hoped might find their way to my hotel. In fact, I had announced toward the end of the show the name of my hotel and gave my room number, but I received no late-night visitors.

After the performance, though, there was one woman at my celebratory dinner who might have come to my hotel room with me. She was an athletic-looking brunette with blood-red cheeks, and after she drank a few beers, she was rubbing my thigh under the table, which I might have enjoyed, but I found her breath to be vomitous. I don't know what she had been eating earlier in the day, but I felt as if my eyelids were going to melt from the acidic nature of her halitosis. Also her personality was halitotic. She said to me, "Is everybody in New York in *therapy?*" But this wasn't intended as a question, it was meant to be a put-down.

"No, everyone in New York *is* a therapist," I said. "Going to therapy was a seventies thing. Being a therapist is what is de rigeur now."

"Well, we don't believe in therapy here," she said.

"Oh, that's good," I said. "Any holocausts in your family history?"

But this didn't phase her, the hand still stroked my thigh, though I wondered if she thought it was odd that I was breathing through my mouth. I might have bedded her, but I love to kiss and she must have had nineteen garlic wiener schnitzels that afternoon, and you can't hit a home run with someone if you don't want to hit a single.

The next morning, I left Heidelberg quite early and took an eight-hour train through the Alps to Venice, Italy, where through international literary contacts I had a free room waiting for me at Hotel La Fenice et Des Artistes. This hotel is named after the famous Venetian playhouse Teatro La Fenice, which is right next door. I was told that Woody Allen, mentioned above, stays at this hotel when he comes to Venice.

But I didn't stay in Woody's suite. I was given a tiny room with no view, but the price, obviously, was reasonable. And the staff of the hotel was quite fascinating. On the walls of the lobby are black-and-white cast photos from shows at La Fenice from the past thirty years, and I realized that two of the older night clerks had been actors in those productions. It gave the place a homey and *The Shining* sort of ambience. There was also a wonderfully maternal seventy-something woman who served me breakfast each morning, and I adored her because she was kind to me.

Venice is the most melancholy, beautiful, and surreal city in the world. It provokes in me a yearning for romance. When I was first there in 1984 as a dreamy twenty-year-old, I swore that I would only return if I was with someone I loved. I failed to keep my vow; I came with someone I have mixed emotions about—myself—but I'd like to make that vow again, though it is pathetic. But traveling does this to me; it's so annoying, it makes me believe in romance, in the possibility of union with a kindred soul. Usually I am happy just going about my business of being nervous and afraid and reading books, and I don't think of sharing this brief life with another, but then you wander around Europe, not worrying about paying your rent for a few weeks, and suddenly you wish that there was someone whose hand you could be holding, whose eyes would look upon the beautiful things that you look upon, someone whom you could need and not be ashamed to need, and someone whom you could comfort and kiss so as to protect them against all of life's slings and arrows.

What mush. But I probably half-believe it. And it's good to try to write mush once in a while, like practicing scales on a piano.

Anyway, one shouldn't go to Venice alone. The beauty is too overwhelming and upsetting. I spent three days there wandering around like a ghost with his heart in his mouth. I spoke to no one but my own mind, though I did have my Chandler novels, which I was rereading for the first time in about ten years. So whenever I'd get too lonely, I'd open up the Chandler and let Philip Marlowe sing to me. Marlowe was my only friend.

Venice is broken up into *sestieri* and I mostly hung around the Dorsoduro *sestiere,* which is the students' quarter and not at all touristy. On the edge of the Dorsoduro there's this lengthy promenade along the very wide waterway Canale Della Guideca, which opens up to the Adriatic. And while you stroll along the promenade, this thin white fog surrounds you and out on the water there are ships, going somewhere, doing something, which gives one the sense that the world has meaning, or at least commerce.

It was chilly when I was in Venice, but not too bad, and I'd take breaks from walking along the promenade and I'd sit on a bench and clutch my coat to my neck and just stare at the water, at the small, insistent waves. And then when I'd get too cold, there were plenty of cheap student restaurants and cafés to warm up in. Italy has the greatest food in the world. Even the little sandwiches that all the cafés sell are delicious—they're filled with cheeses, smoked fish, and all kinds of ham that this Jewish boy loved indulging in— and so I'd eat sandwiches all day long and drink espressos. And then at night I'd have my big meal.

But at night a bad thing would happen to me in Venice. I'd sit in the restaurants and then the student cafés afterward and I would crave alcohol. I'm the first to admit that I'm a dipsomaniac, but I'm only a dipsomaniac when I actually imbibe spirits. Sober I'm simply a maniac or simply dippy or simply boring, but all these are much more manageable states of being than what happens to me as a result of intoxication, which is hospitalizations, liver problems, and having to move back home with my parents.

Still, like most sots, I romanticize booze, and so I was sitting there in the Dorsoduro every night wishing I could have a glass of red wine, as if one glass would turn my life into a Fitzgerald novel. But I didn't drink.

Then my last evening in Venice, I ate my big meal and at the end there was a large fruit cup. I took one spoonful and then a second and it occurred to me that the fruit was soaked in something that tasted quite familiar. I sensed what it was but wasn't entirely certain, so I took a third experimental spoonful and was convinced— sure enough, the fruit was in a bath of wine! But wanting to be thoroughly scientific, I proceeded to have two more experimental spoonfuls. It was most certainly alcohol! Then like a good and outraged temperance society member, I summoned my waiter and pointed at the fruit cup and said accusingly, *"Vino?"*

"*Sì,*" he said, and I gestured with a wave of my hand that he should take away the offending fruit cup and he did. But the damage was done. I felt this most pleasing sensation in the center of my brain and my whole face flushed quite nicely. Liquor hadn't passed these lips in almost three years, and those little spoonfuls of booze to my pure bloodstream were like hits of crack. It was lovely. I thought of throwing in the sober towel and getting a real drink, but I willed myself back to my hotel and crawled into bed with Marlowe, my friend, my lover.

The next day, I temporarily put the fruit cup incident out of my mind and in the morning I explored the Jewish ghetto of Venice, which is the oldest ghetto in the world because it's where the word itself originated. When Ashkenazi Jews came to Venice, they were only allowed to stay in this one area, which was named *geto* and which was where munitions were manufactured and thus was an undesirable place to live. But these German-speaking Jews couldn't pronounce *geto* with a proper Italian accent, so they made it sound like *ghetto,* and a new word was born.

So after my excellent tour of the ghetto's old synagogues, I left Venice and took a train to Florence. During the train ride, I kept thinking about that fruit cup, like a first kiss that I was playing over and over in my mind. It was maddening.

At the station in Florence, I grabbed a tourist map and dragged my bag for about a mile in a rainstorm to a cheap hotel I had read about in my guidebook. And being in noisy Florence with its scooters and cars, I realized how incredibly silent Venice is, that an essential part of its magic is its quiet. It is a city without automobiles. A city where the only way to get around is to walk or take a boat.

I could have used a boat now in Florence—it was an incredible downpour—but I made it to the hotel, though I was completely drenched since I didn't have an umbrella. My room was high-ceilinged and dreary, but I was glad to be out of the rain.

I took a long nap and when I woke up I was quite hungry. It was around eight o'clock at night and still coming down. I put my wet shoes back on and went looking for a restaurant I had read about, but the streets of Florence are narrow and dark and I became a little lost and was again soaked. I ducked in a doorway and I really wanted a drink. I thought of the way my face had flushed the night before. I was in a miserable position. Here I was so lucky to be on the vacation I had been longing for, a vacation that most people would die to take, but it was turning out to be a disaster and I felt like a fool. It was typical hubris. I had been so proud to go on a trip to Europe. But I guess I had been too proud. That will always do you in. Too much pride and you get slammed in the jaw. So my pride had turned into terrible loneliness and despair and a constant, morbid craving for alcohol. My mind was shouting for me to drink. It was painful to want something so bad. It was like there was a pressure in my temples, a teakettle that wouldn't shut up.

I emerged out of the doorway and the next thing I saw was a bar. I looked in the window and a woman smiled at me, or so I thought. I walked past the bar, but I was doomed. Three steps later, I turned around, went into the bar, and the woman who smiled at me immediately left. But that was of no consequence. There was another beautiful woman at the bar drinking a red wine. I sat next to her and ordered the same. I couldn't take it anymore. The wine came, I looked at it for a moment—what was going to happen to me? And then I lifted the glass and had my first drink in nearly three years. I waited for the face flush or pleasure in the center of the brain, but I experienced neither sensation. Then the beautiful woman next to me went and sat at a table. I had thought she was going to be my future wife. I drank the whole glass and nothing happened. So then I ordered a little carafe of grappa since I had been reading about grappa so much in my guidebook.

The grappa did it. Two sips of grappa and I was loaded and the pressure was finally off. I felt that click that Tennessee Williams wrote about in *Cat on a Hot Tin Roof*. Thank God it had come. Everything was now all right. I wasn't miserable anymore. I had my journal and my Chandler in my large coat pockets and I took them out. I sipped my grappa and read and sometimes wrote about the barmaid in front of me. All my journals for years are filled with descriptions of waitresses. Some people note landscapes. I note waitresses.

So, in sprawled, messy writing, here's what I jotted down sitting at that bar: "She is so beautiful. I'm drunk. The dent at the bottom of her neck is perfect. Drunk again. Am I doomed? Black hair parted in the middle, white flawless skin, sad eyelids, red flower mouth, gray V-neck sweater, hint of tiny breasts, black skirt, full womanly ass. She's what the Masters were painting. They loved her. I love her. She's the belladonna. This grappa is hitting me hard. Now there's a white unlit cigarette in her mouth. Now the hair is down. Oh, God, she's a vision. To look at a face like that with love and love returned—what would that be like?"

Drunken mush. So after the grappa, I staggered out of the bar. The girl was too beautiful, I was going to disintegrate in her presence, and so I found my restaurant and had a very good meal, which I washed down with a bottle of wine. Then I went back to my room and had bad drunken sleep, but was quite happy that I hadn't blacked out or vomited. Maybe I wasn't a dipsomaniac anymore.

The next day, I was hungover, but I called up a friend of a friend. A woman. We met for lunch and she spoke wonderful English. It was my first conversation with someone in five days, which isn't that long, but compared to my New York life an eternity. During lunch, I only had a few glasses of wine, since I had cured my dipsomania and was now someone traveling through Europe who could drink like a gentleman. I got a crush on this woman and she seemed smitten with me as well. Her name was Giulia and she was tall and she had blond hair that was the color of wet sand. She had green eyes and funny, imperfect teeth, which I thought were beautiful.

After lunch, she kissed me good-bye and told me to call her that evening, that perhaps we could have dinner. She then went back to work at the publishing company she owns and runs, and I climbed up into the hills above Florence and the sun was out, and from my elevation, the city and all its churches seemed to glow.

That night I did have dinner at Giulia's apartment, but unfortunately, a girlfriend of hers called at the last moment and joined us. Still, it was very pleasant. Giulia's apartment was an enormous duplex with a spectacular view of the Arno, the river that courses through Florence. We had a lovely meal and I drank about a bottle, but again was a perfectly well-behaved gentleman. I also had some port that Giulia brought out especially for me. At the end of the night, I had to leave when the friend left, there was no polite way around it, but after we kissed good-bye, Giulia leaned back against the wall and said huskily, "It's been so lovely meeting you today."

I was thrilled by this; I was falling for her. She was classy and beautiful. She told me to call her the next night. So the whole next day as I tramped around Florence looking at paintings and drinking espressos, I imagined that I was on the verge of romance with a real Florentine. So I called her that night and she said, "Jonathan, something has come up and I'm leaving tonight for a week. Perhaps I'll see you in New York."

"Sure," I said, and we exchanged addresses and then we rang off. I was brokenhearted. During dinner the night before she had alluded to a broken affair with a man in Rome, but it must have been back on. But the whole thing anyway had been a delusion on my part, something to keep me going, and now I was back to being alone and miserable. So the old dipsomaniac decided it was time to make an appearance. It had only been a matter of time. I started off with several pints of beer and then drank a bottle of wine during dinner, and so then, good and drunk, I tramped out to La Cascine, this park, where I had read in my guidebook that transvestite prostitutes could be found at night.

On my way there, I stopped at a concession stand and bought a pack of cigarettes and three cans of beer, which I put in my pockets, and then I finally came to the road that went through the park. The road where the transvestites stood in the shadows by the trees. I was back with my people! This is where I belong, I thought, not with the Giulias of the world. I can't make it with the Giulias. Too classy.

So like one of the hookers, I leaned against a tree in the darkness and sipped beers and smoked cigarettes. I watched the men pull up in their little Italian cars and the transvestites would approach and sometimes disappear with the men if negotiations were successful. I always like watching these things, and it's the same everywhere in the world—this haggling over money with whores. And I felt at peace. I was standing in mud from all the rain. I could smell it. I was part of the earth. So much of the time I worry about getting into trouble, but then when I am in trouble, I feel good because I'm not worrying about it anymore.

A hooker approached me. She was tall and wore a dark wig. She had a black miniskirt and a leather jacket. She was kind of husky, and her makeup was as thick as a small phone book. But she had nice eyes.

"*Buona sera, signoria,*" I said and sipped my beer.

She said something I didn't catch, which I think meant blowjob because she added a sucking motion with her fist aimed at her mouth.

"No, *grazie,*" I said.

Then she got right in front of me and dragged her thumb along my eyebrows, which are somewhat albinish and often curious to people. "*Bèllo,*" she said, which was very tender, and I liked having my eyebrows stroked. Then she grabbed my wrist playfully but hard—she was quick—and somehow the miniskirt was up and she put my hand on her cock. The thing wasn't erect but was remarkably thick, and in the dim light I got a glimpse of it—uncircumcised.

She smiled at me with allure. "No, *grazie,*" I said with politesse, and she let go of my hand and then traced her thumb along my eyebrows again and walked off with style, a swing of her hips.

An odd laugh came out of me. Then, making sure she wasn't looking, I poured my beer on my hand to disinfect it. I figured the highlight of my evening had occurred, so I began to stagger home. I passed a disco at the beginning of the park where young beautiful girls, eighteen- and nineteen-year-olds, were jumping over puddles to get to the entrance. I loved watching them do that. These little leaps of their beautiful legs.

Then I walked along the Arno, finished off the rest of my beer, and thought of jumping in. Not a serious thought, but the rushing orange-brown water looked inviting. It would be like a sudden yet violent sleep.

I made it back to the hotel. In the morning I was sick, my eyes were jaundiced and swimming in bile, but I felt better in a way. I knew I had to get back on the water wagon. I had twelve days left on my trip and I wanted to survive them. There were things I had to be alive for: my friends, my parents, my son.

That afternoon I went and saw Michelangelo's David. His uncircumcised penis looked exactly like the sweet transvestite's. I wrote in my journal, "I have only two Italian penises to go by, but I think they are of an unusual thickness when flaccid."

ABOUT THE AUTHOR

JONATHAN AMES is the author of two novels, *The Extra Man* and *I Pass Like Night,* and is a columnist for the *New York Press*. He is the winner of a Guggenheim Fellowship and a Transatlantic Review Award. In addition to writing, he performs frequently as a storyteller in theaters and nightclubs. His one-man show of storytelling, *Oedipussy,* debuted off-off-Broadway in 1999. Jonathan Ames is also a retired amateur boxer; he fought under the nickname "The Herring Wonder."